FiftyYears of the
GREEN LINE

Fifty Years of the
GREEN LINE

Kenneth Warren

LONDON
IAN ALLAN LTD

First published 1980

ISBN 0 7110 1029 3

© Ian Allan Ltd 1980

Published by Ian Allan Ltd, Shepperton, Surrey;
and printed by Ian Allan Printing Ltd at their works
at Coombelands in Runnymede, England

Contents

Preface

Green Line coaches have been a familiar part of the London transport scene for 50 years. Though the identity of the service has been maintained, the history of its development, successes and vicissitudes has not so far been examined except in small segments; this book is an attempt to survey half a century of organisational change. At one stage in the writing, it appeared that this account might be an obituary; fortunately at the eleventh hour came a revival and the coaches now in operation are running as well as they have ever done in the last 20 years. The semi-fast suburban coach running daily, throughout the year, at regular intervals, on which the passenger pays his fare as he boards, is a

facility that flourishes only in London; there are express workings elsewhere, of course, but they have never been as extensively developed as Green Line.

A book of this nature relies very much on published material and other sources. There are sometimes conflicts of evidence and date which I have tried to resolve without recourse to long discussion. A particular difficulty, for example, has been the question of withdrawals of services. Should the withdrawal date be the first date on which the service did not run at all, or should it be the date on which the service last operated? I have aimed for consistency by opting for the latter. There may be errors of fact and interpretation in this account, though I hope they are few; however many there may be they are my responsibility and I hope my readers will let me know what they are.

I am much indebted to Mr John Parke, editor of *Buses*, who very kindly put me in touch with a number of those concerned with Green Line either professionally or as enthusiasts (or both, of course). Foremost, I would like to thank Mr R. S. Turnbull who read the first drafts, made many helpful comments and gave much encouragement; I am most grateful for his support. Mr D. W. K. Jones kindly provided me with detailed information on vehicles; Mr George Dickins recalled his wartime planning for the services that began in 1946. I have had access to several photographic collections and would wish to express my thanks to Mr Jones, Mr George Robbins and to the Reverend Edward Shirras; the staff of the London Transport photographic library have been unfailingly helpful. I am most grateful to many others for less formal help – to the Green Line crews I have had words with over the years, and to friends whose travel experiences have been passed on to me.

This book is dedicated to all those who have been responsible for keeping Green Line on the road; I hope they and their passengers find it of interest.

Kenneth Warren
September 1979

Left: The 10T10 coach exemplified the dignity, style and reliability that were features of Green Line journeys in the late 1930s and after the war. *London Transport*

GREEN LINE

To us, distraught with frost in a white waste,
    The Green Line came as the Leviathan moves
Ponderous and sure, and stood to our command.
    And the great door rolled back along its
        polished grooves.

Past hope relieved, we clambered in and laid
    On steel-sprung seats the burden of our cares.
The tall conductor took his tickets down
    And rode the plunging deck to take our
        proffered fares.

The ice-bound roads roared dully underneath
    Our moving world of still and steamy heat.
We telescoped our necks like sleepy hens,
    And let the white world rip, and thawed our
        frozen feet.

The long bus rode the ridges down, and took
    The thunder in its springs; and as it went
The tall conductor twanged his ringing punch
    And whistled from the deeps of unexplored
        content.

                P. M. Hubbard.
Punch 7 February 1951. Reproduced by permission of the Editor.

1 The Background

The decade which started in 1920 was an era of enterprise and expansion in the bus industry comparable with the 1840–1850 Railway Mania, and the causes were very much the same. Technical development was rapid, mechanical reliability of vehicles was assured, and a great field was open to advance and speculation. By 1929 the present operating companies or their forebears had established their spheres of influence, and the coming of the motorbus to the countryside was part of a social revolution that linked urban and rural communities in ways of life and thought.

The road established itself in the popular imagination after a demise of a century or so since the stage coaches had given way to the railways. It became the fashion 'to go by road', whether the vehicle was a motorcoach or the diminutive Austin 7. The unhappy state of the railway companies was only one factor; it would be unjust to level a general criticism of ineptitude against the managements who had to contend with periods of labour difficulty, years of coal shortage and the effects of poor maintenance during the war. Additionally, the grouping of the railway companies in 1921 had lost considerable loyalty that attached to the smaller operations. However, the fact remains that the railways could not effectively compete with the road motor and a rather dogged struggle between the two forms of transport began. Only the Southern Railway, under the management of Sir Herbert Walker, showed significant initiative and electric trains became increasingly part of the suburban scene.

Thus, coach services to the seaside and to principal towns and cities were well established by the mid-1920s, and if the coaches were rather small by current standards, they were reasonably comfortable and cheap to travel in. Further, all operators made great play of their concern for their passengers and this concern was made manifest by the relationship drivers built up with their customers. Every year saw more ambitious plans by the companies, more routes opened and more people travelling and the period culminated in the setting up of the London Coastal Coaches organisation and the building of the imposing coach station at Victoria.

It is quite clear from the statements of Lord Ashfield, Chairman and Managing Director, and by its preoccupation with bus operation that the London General Omnibus Company (henceforth LGOC) was not interested in long-distance coach work. Its central activity remained operating stage-carriage services in London, an activity regulated since the London Traffic Act (1924) by the Metropolitan Police who were made responsible for licensing vehicles and routes. Some LGOC buses already ran beyond the Metropolitan Police District – as early as 1914 regular services were running from Golders Green to St Albans, for example, and Sundays only routes were extended to Dorking, Maidenhead and Epping. The LGOC had concerned itself at an early stage with defining its boundaries and spheres of influence and had secured its operations in out-London districts by means of operating agreements.

However, Lord Ashfield became concerned towards the end of the 1920s by the loss of earnings on these longer routes caused by the running of excursions by small companies from London to centres like Windsor and Epping. Some out-London companies running regular services to and from the coast began inserting fare stages within the LGOC specified area from 1927. Further, enterprising operators, usually small companies with two or three vehicles, saw the possibilities of profitable journeys (on a fast or semi-fast basis) which served places away from the railway lines, or even near them where existing rail services were inadequate or unattractive. They

saw also a loophole in the 1924 Act that allowed them to run if they initiated services outside the Metropolitan Police District and relied solely on local licences, often easily obtained from local Watch Committees. The legal issues were never settled despite frequent protests from the LGOC to the Minister of Transport. To the threats from the Independents on the London streets were added the threats arising from uncontrolled operations within its own area but just outside the limits of Metropolitan Police control; the LGOC saw its position being rapidly eroded.

Having perceived the possibilities, shrewd

Top: Thackrays' Way, actually the Ledbury Transport Co Ltd of Reading, were early on the Reading to London roads and operated via Slough and via Ascot from mid-1929. The Gilford coach was an example of the 166SD type which seated 26 passengers. Thackrays' Way withdrew the Ascot route in 1931. The roof luggage rack on the coach was a standard feature of the time. *George Robbins Collection*

Above: Skylark purchased Gilfords for their services from Hertford to Guildford and from London to High Wycombe. This vehicle is another of the 166SD type (indicating a wheelbase of 16ft 6in and standard drive) which was an extremely popular model with independent operators. It became a member of London Transport's GF class but did not remain in service for very long.
George Robbins Collection

operators acted quickly. Thus, services initiated in 1927 included the Redcar route from Tunbridge Wells (beginning 16 September), Glenton running from London to Sevenoaks in the same month and Priest's operation from London to Luton which began in November. In 1928 the pace of development increased dramatically and services were opened to Oxford (3 March, Red and Black Coaches), Bedford (7 March, Constant's Super-deluxe Coaches), Aylesbury (19 May, West London Coaches and in August, Red Rover). In October Strawhatter opened a Luton to Kings Cross service, Baldock Motor Transport Co (later Queen Line) worked Biggleswade, Baldock and London; Birch Brothers began Aldwych to Hatfield and Bedford in November followed in December by Imperial Motor Services (Priest again) on the same road. Hillman started work on the Brentwood road in December – a significant operator, this – and, also important in the history of Green Line, the Skylark Motor Coach Co Ltd began an Oxford Circus to Guildford route on 23 December.

In almost all cases vehicles operated on a regular interval basis and picked up passengers without the necessity of pre-booking. Fare scales were attractive in that they undercut existing rates for rail travel and from the first operators emphasised their care for the passenger. This was a period when passengers could be picked up and could alight at will and concern for their interests once they were

on board was made explicit. The motor coach of the day exemplified the very latest technology; in comparison many railway vehicles were museum pieces. The firms were small firms with some claim to local status and the image was established of private enterprise competing more than effectively with the near-monopoly of the giant LGOC and with the remote railway managements.

In 1929 independent companies opened 30 or more services to Central London; these included the Grimwood Parlour Coaches run from Egham (February), the Enterprise Coaches service (later Bucks Express) from Watford (26 September) and Skylark services to High Wycombe (14 September), Hertford (4 December) – linked with the existing Guildford route – and to Dorking (also 4 December). The services were vigorously marketed, changed or adapted according to public need,

and were altogether more flexible operations than the regulated buses of the LGOC. Some flourished and survived, others disappeared after a few weeks. Purchase of successful services also changed the names of the operators from time to time. The whole activity, unregulated, adaptable, furiously competitive, aroused the alarm of the LGOC, the Metropolitan Police, the Ministry of Transport and some members of the public who looked upon this display of private enterprise as nothing more than wasteful competition. In 1930 another 36 or so services were opened by independent operators. By then, however, the LGOC had itself joined in, the 1930 Road Traffic Act was about to become law and the whole London coach business was about to become the subject of a public enquiry. The vehicles of many types and liveries that milled around Oxford Circus and lined up along the Embankment were about to be regularised, restricted and coordinated.

The intervention into the semi-fast coach business by the LGOC was forced on the organisation which – unprotected in this field by the 1924 Act – had to compete in order to protect its own interests. Lord Ashfield's strategy was twofold; an Express Department was established within the LGOC itself, and secondly companies that had long had agreements with the LGOC were brought into closer association and given responsibility for initiating and operating coach services. It can be seen that the Express Depart-

ment was set up only as an interim move; as soon as possible all coach operation was transferred outside the centre and into the Country area.

The most important company operating south of the LGOC was undoubtedly the East Surrey Traction Co Ltd which, incorporated as a private company on 16 March 1911, began running between Redhill and Reigate on 23 May the same year. Its secretary, A. H. Hawkins, later became General Manager and was a key figure in the London Country area until his retirement in 1946. In an age when personality counted in transport affairs, the name of A. H. Hawkins is inevitably linked with the creation of Green Line. East Surrey had made an 'area agreement' with the LGOC on 26 January 1914; this agreement on operating boundaries was renewed on 7 July 1921 and the closer links with the London company were evidenced by the acquisition of LGOC-type buses and equipment. In 1928 East Surrey gained control of Autocar Services Ltd of Tunbridge Wells – a firm dating from 1909 – and was itself bought out by LGOC in 1929. By this time it was operating 169 buses over 33 routes (apart from the Autocar services) and had reached points as far apart as Dartford and Guildford. It had already tried out an express operation between Redhill Reigate and Oxford Circus in 1928, an early example of an A. H. Hawkins initiative.

North of the Thames the most significant operator was the National Omnibus and Transport

11

Co, reconstituted on 13 February 1920 from the Clarkson Steam Car firm that had had interests in vehicle building and operation in many places since 1902. An area agreement was signed with LGOC in 1921 and a range of services using London-type vehicles was built up based on garages in Watford, Hatfield, Ware, Bishops Stortford, Luton and Romford. The Hertford and District Motor Co was acquired in 1924 and the garage at the Town Hall, Ware was transferred to National ownership. The parent company split into sections on 28 February 1929 and buses ran from that date under the title Eastern National. From the point of view of association with the LGOC, however, the title National was retained.

Finally, Amersham and District, a company first registered in 1919, came under LGOC financial control on 26 August 1929. So far as the travelling public was concerned, however, the 43 buses based at Amersham itself and at High Wycombe remained independent until 1933.

Thus, with its own organisation ready – through its Express Department – and by its agreements with and control of companies to the north and south, LGOC was poised to enter the coach business. Watford to Golders Green opened on 2 October 1929, as detailed later; East Surrey as operating agents started operations from Reigate, Redhill and Dorking on 6 June 1930, and Autocar from Tunbridge Wells on the same day. There came a need to identify these services and to set up a company to provide capital for vehicles and buildings. Lord Ashfield's suggestion of 'Green Line' did not at first win the acclaim of A. H.

Hawkins, but he changed his mind having recognised the relevance of the image. The company, Green Line Coaches Ltd, was registered on 9 July 1930 with a capital of £20,000: a wholly-owned subsidiary of the LGOC. Lord Ashfield became chairman, Frank Pick a director and A. H. Hawkins managing director. Red Line, Blue Line and Yellow Line companies were also registered to protect the names, but they were never used.

Development of the road services is considered in detail in the next Chapter, but some reference to subsequent changes of organisation would complete the picture. East Surrey Traction Co Ltd became London General Country Services Ltd on 25 January 1932 as a preliminary to taking over LGOC interests in the National Omnibus and Transport Co Ltd on 1 March 1932. With the implementation of the London Passenger Transport Act on 1 July 1933, London General Country Services and Green Line Coaches were vested in the new London Passenger Transport Board. Autocar Services, being outside the designated area, were transferred to Maidstone and District Motor Services Ltd. Amersham and District became part of the LPTB Country Bus section on 24 November 1933, though completion of purchase was made on 1 October.

Below: The LGOC's incursion into express operation is exemplified by this presentation shot of one of the first series of T-type coaches in the red and black livery worn by the first 40 vehicles in the class. This coach was based at Alpha Street, Slough, and worked between Charing Cross and Windsor. The service began on 20 April 1930 and passed to Green Line after the company was set up on 9 July 1930. *London Transport*

2 The Foundations of Green Line

Having committed itself to the fray the LGOC, through its Private Hire Department, inaugurated a service on 2 October 1929 to run between Watford (Market Street) and Golders Green, through fares being made available on the Underground to Central London stations. Coaches, vehicles extracted from the Private Hire fleet, ran every 15 minutes via Bushey, Mill Hill and Hendon. Somewhat mysteriously to the public eye, operations ceased on 12 November after some six weeks; this apparent failure of nerve has never been satisfactorily explained. Then, on 18 December the Company reopened the Watford to Golders Green route and, in addition, initiated a service from Watford to Charing Cross Embankment via Oxford Circus. This represented a much firmer commitment, and Private Hire vehicles, garaged at Leavesden Road, Watford and at Brixton Hill, continued on these services until the arrival of the T-type coach.

The Watford to Golders Green Service, publicised as a General/Underground Motorcoach and Rail service, settled down to run every 30 minutes during the day, every hour in the evenings, taking 33 minutes over the journey. The longer route to the Embankment at first ran every 40 minutes, adjusted to every 30 minutes in May 1930. Allowed 70 minutes for the through journey, the coaches were very approximately timed at intermediate points; however, the timetable leaflet of 14 June, headed 'General Express Coach' indicated more exact timings.

The next venture came with the opening of a Charing Cross to Windsor via Slough service by the new Express Coach Department on 20 April 1930. Coaches – T-type vehicles in red and black livery – ran every 30 minutes between the Embankment and The Lord Raglan in Windsor, via Hyde Park Corner and Hammersmith. Much of the

Below: T122 appears in the first livery adopted by Green Line Coaches Ltd and is one of the first series of coaches with a 27-seat, rear-entrance body. The position of the emergency door was an indentifying feature of the type. The roof boards are of early design, indicating the places served; route letters were added in 1931. *London Transport*

Left: Interior view of the first series of T-type coach, looking towards the rear. The luxury of the fittings might be noted though the design was not enhanced by the fussy curtains. The vehicle is classified as a Metropolitan Stage Carriage and is licensed to carry 27 passengers. The tip-up seat by the door was seldom used by the conductor whose role demanded that he stood most of the time. *London Transport*

Right: The garage in London Road, Staines, in 1931 shortly after the erection of the corrugated iron shed. Two first series T-type coaches are being prepared for service. The untidy nature of the environment needs no comment. Timetables have been affixed to the more secure section of the outer fence. *London Transport*

road was already covered by the long established bus route 81. The Express Department coaches, however, carried no route number (or letter) but had the terminal and intermediate points painted on the louvre windows. The destination was indicated at the front and additionally a neat wooden board was affixed to the back. The vehicles for this service were garaged at Alpha Street, Slough. The next development was the opening of a Charing Cross to Windsor route via Shepherds Bush, Bedfont and Staines, every 30 minutes, on 10 July 1930.

Green Line Coaches Ltd had been registered the previous day, 9 July, but much service development was left in the hands of the LGOC, at least so far as the travelling public was concerned. Thus on 23 July Express Department coaches (released from the Watford services, transferred to Green Line on 17 July) initiated a service from Charing Cross to Sunningdale via Hounslow and Staines, where the newly-built garage was situated. London routeing was via Bush House, Trafalgar Square, Piccadilly and Hyde Park Corner. Initially every hour, the service was increased to every 30 minutes from 30 July, to become every hour again with the opening of an Oxford Circus to Ascot service on 3 September, operating every 60 minutes. A

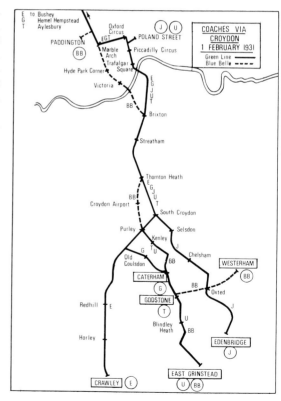

30-minute service was thus available from Hyde Park Corner to Virginia Water.

Meanwhile, on 2 August, the Express Department opened a service from Charing Cross to Maidenhead, running every 30 minutes and basing the coaches at Maidenhead itself. The next changes involved the formal transfer of the LGOC services to Green Line; thus the Ascot and Sunningdale services were taken over on 1 October (and subsequently diverted via Ashford and Feltham on 29 November); the Windsor via Staines route was turned over to Green Line on 1 October also, the Slough routes to Windsor and to Maidenhead following on 18 October. The opportunity was taken with this last change of closing the garage accommodation at Maidenhead, transferring the base to Alpha Street, Slough and interworking the Windsor and Maidenhead departures to provide four per hour to Windsor and two to Maidenhead. The Express Department was at this point wound up; all further coach developments were ostensibly Green Line, based on out-London garages.

Four services began on 6 June 1930. Autocar Services Ltd opened an Oxford Circus to Tunbridge Wells route to run every 60 minutes. East Surrey began running hourly from Reigate to Oxford Circus via Sutton, and every 30 minutes from Redhill to Oxford Circus via Purley. Dorking to Oxford Circus via Morden was opened on the same day, every 60 minutes from the beginning; coaches for this route were garaged initially at Reigate, later at Leatherhead. The services from Tunbridge Wells, Reigate and Dorking were increased to every 30 minutes on 24 June. The Redhill service was subsequently extended to Crawley (every hour) on 12 November.

East Surrey were provided with 12 T-type coaches for the services started on 6 June; the vehicles were in the LGOC colours, ie red and black with a grey roof. 'East Surrey' was carried on the sides and in the front indicator. The arrival of five more coaches allowed the increased frequencies announced for 24 June.

Next followed services from Godstone Green via Kenley to Oxford Circus (every 30 minutes) on 29 September (using East Surrey all-weather Regals), and Great Bookham to Oxford Circus via Leatherhead and Morden, again every 30 minutes, on 1 October. Coaches based at Dunton Green began running hourly from Westerham to Oxford Circus via The Elephant and Great Scotland Yard on 8 October. Subsequently this service was extended to Sevenoaks, White Hart. On 22 October East Surrey began the Oxted and Chel-

15

sham service, coaches running every 120 minutes from the outer terminus, every 30 minutes from Chelsham. Coaches on this route, based at Chelsham, were LGOC all-weather Reliances, hired to East Surrey and bearing the Green Line fleet name. On 6 December the service was extended to Edenbridge and improved to hourly beyond Chelsham. The East Grinstead to Oxford Circus route began on 12 November, coaches running every hour.

Thus nine services were initiated by Autocar and East Surrey between them within six months – a remarkable example of enterprise and planning. Some 42 vehicles were deployed and crewing them employed some 220 men.

As operating agents for the LGOC, National began a coach service from Welwyn Garden City to Charing Cross on 17 September 1930. Coaches, based in Welwyn and in Green Line livery, travelled every 30 minutes via Hatfield, Barnet, Golders Green and Oxford Circus. On 1 October the Bishops Stortford to Charing Cross service began, coaches being based at South Street, Bishops Stortford. The route taken was via Epping, Woodford, Walthamstow and Tottenham and a half-hourly service was provided. An interesting feature of National operations was their reluctance to use the term 'timetable' – leaflets, with neat green covers, were known as 'Working Schedules'.

A service from Hertford was inaugurated on 22 November, coaches leaving every hour for Ponders End, Enfield and Charing Cross. The vehicles were garaged at Ware. All National coach services were regarded as Green Line, National being the operating agents, so designated on publicity material.

Registered on 9 July 1930, the first service operated by the Green Line company in its own right was Charing Cross to Guildford, via Bush House, Trafalgar Square, Oxford Circus, Hammer-

Above: Staines garage, second stage, later in 1931. The shaky fence has gone and 'Green Line Coaches' is writ large on the shed. The timetable board is headed 'Green Line and General Routes', and the first vehicle in view is an ADC coach, notable for its long nose and sunshine roof. *London Transport*

Above right: A second series T awaits departure at Limehill Road, Tunbridge Wells when the Coach Station was still in Autocar hands. There are few passengers about — perhaps surprisingly, considering the 3/10d (19p) return fare to London. *London Transport*

smith, Barnes, Malden and Esher, Coaches began running every 30 minutes on 17 July. Next came the Brentwood service on 23 July; this ran from Charing Cross via Aldgate every 20 minutes throughout the day, every 15 minutes from 23 September. Coaches were based initially at commercial premises in North Street, Romford. A service from Tring to Charing Cross was initiated on 8 September, coaches – based at Leavesden Road, Watford – running every 30 minutes. There were boarding restrictions on this route between Bushey and Watford, Watford Corporation as licensing authority seeking to limit journeys along the High Street. Next, on 20 September, began the Harpenden (Church Green) to Charing Cross service, every 30 minutes via Radlett, Golders Green and Oxford Circus. The providing garage for this service appears to have been the Comfy Cars garage at Harpenden which was quoted as an Enquiry Office on the timetable literature. October 11 saw the beginning of the Charing Cross to Chertsey service, operated via Hammersmith, Richmond and Weybridge. The service interval was the by now almost standard 30 minutes.

The next significant event was the joining of four services to provide cross-London routes on 10 December. Thus, the Reigate to Oxford Circus coaches now ran through to Welwyn Garden City

over the National road (except in the evenings, when coaches commenced journeys at Northumberland Avenue or Oxford Circus, overlapping between these two points). The Great Bookham service was put through to Harpenden, the evening London terminal arrangements being much the same as on the Reigate to Welwyn route. These cross-London workings were the only ones realised of a large-scale plan drawn up by Green Line in November 1930. Apart from the links which were never made, for example Gravesend and Windsor via Central London, Amersham and Sevenoaks – an interesting case of social matching, this – it is worthy of note that Green Line intended serving places that in the event never saw a coach. Thus Orpington has never been on the Green Line map, nor have Harrow Weald, Wheathampstead, Royston and West Wycombe.

The eventful year 1930 ended with the opening of Poland Street Coach Station on 25 December. The Guildford and the Windsor via Staines services were operated immediately into the new terminus which was on the site of a former brewery near Oxford Circus. Getting into and out of the station was not very easy and more traffic movements were generated than had the coaches remained on the main streets. However, these several moves – the opening of the coach station and the development of cross London workings went some way to accommodate the police view that the coaches were causing intolerable traffic congestion around Oxford Circus and along the Embankment. Traffic control and engineering was in its infancy in 1930 and the press of vehicles in Central London caused considerable confusion on the streets. As relative newcomers the coaches were specific targets for criticism that followed frequent hold-ups and jams.

Behind the brief statement that a service had been initiated lay a great deal of complex activity.

From the establishment of priorities came the decision to set up a service from, say, East Grinstead. The management had to be assured, so far as was possible, that such a service would be financially viable; choice of route would be influenced by the number of operators already engaged on it or by the fact that no one had so far established a facility. Adequate garaging accommodation would be another consideration. Route planning was not perhaps as detailed as it would be now, but timings would require calculation and crew rosters drawn up. Staffing at the garages would also need augmenting, though doubtless in the early days existing employees would undertake a considerable amount of overtime working to get the service under way. However, an hourly service from East Grinstead would need four coaches; crew requirements would come to something like 15 drivers and the same number of conductors. Fare stages would need to be drawn up and equitable decisions made as to the level of fare to be charged in the light of existing competition and the current railway fares. A few days before the initiation was due the coaches would arrive for a brief period of driver familiarisation and final mechanical checking. As the Green Line operation developed, doubtless this preliminary period became shorter and shorter. Publicity would be launched by press announcements and distribution of timetable leaflets – sometimes the leaflets were optimistic in that they gave starting dates that could not, in fact, be kept. In one matter, at least, there was no problem: there was no need to provide stop signs in the streets as at this time the coaches could pick up and set down passengers anywhere on the point of route. Finally, on the first day the first coach would pull out onto the road, destination London, Oxford Circus, at the very beginning of a long tradition in road passenger transport that still survives.

3   Control and Coordination

The activities of Green Line, its associates and its rivals, quickly attracted the attention of the authorities, and throughout its period of development the suburban coach business was under threat of Government regulation. The London Traffic Act of 1924 had established a London and Home Counties Traffic Advisory Committee and the attention of this body was drawn to the scenes of confusion in Central London streets caused by the vast influx of coaches. In September 1930 a traffic census revealed that on two Saturdays more than 3,500 coaches were moving in central streets in each direction. As has been noted, Green Line made some accommodating moves by establishing some cross-London routes, thus avoiding 'layovers' at central points, and by opening the coach station in Poland Street.

The 1930 Road Traffic Act made it necessary for an operator to seek a licence for each service it wished to run. Full statements of schedules and fare stages had to be submitted to the Traffic Commissioner (only one for the Metropolitan Police District) and to the Traffic Commissioners in other Traffic Areas; these requirements were in addition to Certificates of Fitness for Public Service Vehicles, and assessment of the fitness of applicants to hold Road Service Licences. Thus Green Line came under the law and applications for licences were initiated. It was clear from the beginning that the granting of licences would be a restrictive policy and operators identified some hostility to the coach in official minds. There has been some suggestion of a railway bias in the Ministry of Transport at the time. A key date was 9 February 1931, after which it was not possible either to initiate a service or to claim 'existing facility' in support of a case for a licence. This explains the extreme haste with which Green Line and other companies put coaches on the roads as the deadline drew near. Services estab-

lished after 9 February were in defiance of the law and quickly withdrawn after the issuing of Ministry Orders.

The Road Traffic Act differentiated between a Stage Carriage licence and an Express Carriage licence. The first required a fare under 1/- (5p), while the second was issued for a route with no fares less than 1/-. Express Carriages were required to carry jacks and first aid equipment. It was clearly an advantage for all Green Line routes to operate under Stage Carriage regulations and each route had at least one fare under the mandatory 1/-. The exception was the service to Whipsnade Zoo which ran with an Express Carriage licence.

Coordination of London's transport was achieved through the London Passenger Transport Act to which – after prolonged Parliamentary battles – the Royal Assent was given on 13 April 1933. The Act came into force on 1 July 1933 and the London Passenger Transport Board took responsibility for all local passenger movement within its designated area, the 'Central' area being made coterminous with the Metropolitan Traffic Area. Some familiar transport men survived the organisational change, notably Lord Ashfield and Frank Pick who served as chairman and vice-chairman of the Board; A. H. Hawkins was appointed general manager of the Country Buses and Coaches and continued his operations at Bell Street, Reigate. This takes the account some way ahead of what was happening on the roads, however, and reference must now be made to the events of January and February 1931.

On 8 January 1931 the Ascot and Sunningdale services, formerly terminating at Charing Cross, were diverted to Poland Street Coach Station, to be followed on 14 January by coaches from Hertford and East Grinstead. Also on 14 January there was a reorganisation of the service to Tring involving a

*Above:*An exterior view of Poland Street Coach Station in January 1931, seemingly on a rather bleak night. The garish architecture, characteristic of the time, contrasts with the dignity of the Victorian lamp-post and tethering posts in the middle of the road. The identity of the ghostly travellers under the lamp is unknown. *London Transport*

Right: The vehicle exit from Poland Street Coach Station. This somewhat sinister view demonstrates the serious lack of space that hampered movement of coaches. This is February 1931 when the second series of T-type coaches (those going to Byfleet and Tunbridge Wells) would have been almost new. *London Transport*

reduction in frequency to hourly and an extension (as a through working) to Godstone Green. This allowed the operation of a new hourly departure from Hemel Hempstead which worked through to Caterham Station. These services were operated from Leavesden Road garage (and Godstone); though running through Watford, a boarding restriction within the town remained, The Red Lion, Bushey, being the first picking-up point south of Watford. Additional journeys were advertised to start from The Red Lion, every 30 minutes, to Redhill and hourly to Crawley, thus establishing a 10-minute service between Bushey and Oxford Circus – a point made by over-printing on the timetable leaflet. These services were advertised as Green Line, in conjunction with East Surrey.

On 15 January the Chertsey service was operated into Poland Street, and the next day the Edenbridge and Dorking coaches followed. Some 16 vehicles an hour were now entering and leaving this somewhat inconveniently-sited terminus, a total increased by four when the Tunbridge Wells and Sevenoaks routes were diverted there on 28 January.

Meanwhile, on 26 January, using five 7T7-type vehicles in their own livery, Amersham and District inaugurated a service between Amersham, Oakfield Corner and Oxford Circus via Gerrards Cross. Coaches ran every hour, carrying the route number 17. The service had been advertised to start on 22 January, and to run to and from Chesham, but doubtless lateness of delivery of vehicles and other considerations modified the original plans. In fact Chesham was reached on 1 February, but the route was cut back to Amersham again on 22 October. Another new service began on 28 January when coaches began running from Ascot and Sunningdale through to Dartford, the London routeing being via Hyde Park Corner,

Above: A first series T-type coach on service V waits at Golders Green for departure time. The route was re-lettered T in October 1933. Stanley Lupino and Jessie Matthews are appearing at the Hippodrome in 'Hold My Hand'.
George Robbins Collection

Great Scotland Yard or Northumberland Avenue and Westminster Bridge. Four vehicles were allocated to Swanley for this service, journeys between the garage and Dartford being timetabled which must have represented quite the earliest and latest facilities between these two points ever provided. Swanley was also responsible for mounting an hourly service from Farningham to Poland Street. These operations were designated East Surrey in the timetable literature.

Three new routes were opened on the same day, 31 January, all running to and from Poland Street. These were services to Rickmansworth via Wembley, to Sunbury Common and to West Byfleet. The Rickmansworth service was initially advertised to run every 30 minutes from the Embankment via Oxford Circus, Piccadilly Circus and Trafalgar Square, but in fact it started at Poland Street. Watford Leavesden Road supplied coaches for this service which was unusual in that passengers boarding in Rickmansworth itself could only do so having pre-booked their tickets; otherwise they were free to board or alight anywhere along the line of route as was customary. The second new service started on 31 January, that to Sunbury Common, ran every 30 minutes via Hammersmith, Richmond and Kingston. With the Chertsey service, four coaches an hour were now available between Kingston and London. This route was originally planned to go via Sloane Square and Putney. The third inauguration, the route to West Byfleet Corner, followed the Guildford road as far as Cobham. Again, a 30-minute service was provided, Addlestone garage allocating six vehicles.

It was clearly intended that Woking should be the terminus of this service, and doubtless local licensing difficulties prevented coaches reaching this point. West Byfleet thus shared the distinction with Great Bookham of being small communities whose existence assumed the high status of appearing on Green Line destination blinds.

Two days before the deadline, on 7 February 1931, the Uxbridge service began, coaches leaving Poland Street every 30 minutes and taking between 56 and 59 minutes for the journey. An hourly extension to Beaconsfield, though advertised, did not run. A curiosity of this service was that the coaches were kept at the AEC works in Southall. They did not, of course, come straight off the production line as the coach-building was done elsewhere, but clearly they were not away for long. The fare table was a curiosity, too: it was almost the ultimate in simplicity, carrying only two fares – 1/- single and 1/6 return.

Green Line began running hourly between the Embankment and The Bell at Upminster via Aldgate, Barking and Becontree on 21 February, increased on 28 to every 30 minutes. This appeared in clear contravention of the Road Traffic Act, though Green Line were not the only operators to test the law – Premier Line started running to Sunbury Common on 22 February. However, the Upminster service was withdrawn on 1 April on the

ROUTE FOLLOWED IN CENTRAL LONDON : Hammersmith Rd., Holland Rd., Holland Park Avenue, Bayswater Rd., Hyde Park St., Connaught St., Edgware Rd., Seymour St., Portman Square, Wigmore St., Regent St.

To LONDON.

MONDAYS TO FRIDAYS.

															Then at minutes past each hour	
Guildford (Horse & Groom) ... dep.	a.m.	a.m.	a.m.	a.m.	a.m.	a.m.	a.m.		p.m.	p.m.	p.m.	p.m.	p.m.	20	50	...
Ripley (Post Office) ...	6 31	7	7 31	8	8 31	9		8 50		5 20	5 34	6 0	6 15	34	...	
West Byfleet Corner ...	6 57	7 25	7 45	8 15												

SATURDAYS.

		Then at minutes past each hour				
	p.m.	p.m.	1	15	31	45
	12 4					

To WEST BYFLEET and GUILDFORD.

MONDAYS TO FRIDAYS.

							Then at minutes past each hour		
London (Poland St. Coach Stn.) dep.	p.m.	10 15					3	48	18
Oxford Circus ...		10 15					58		28
Hammersmith (Greyhound Motors) ...				10 25			5		43
Barnes (Railway Hotel) ...				10 33					
Malden (Cross Roads) ...				10 40					
Tolworth (Ewell Road) ...				10 46					
Esher (Windsor Arms) ...				11					
Cobham (White Lion) ...				11 8					
Byfleet ...				11 21					
West Byfleet Corner ... arr.				11 28					
Ripley (Post Office) ... dep.									
Guildford (Horse & Groom) ... arr.				11 33					

SATURDAYS.

		Then at minutes past each hour		
	p.m.			

To LONDON.

SUNDAYS.

			Then at minutes past each hour		
Guildford (Horse & Groom) ... dep.	a.m.		1	31	
Ripley (Post Office) ...	7 31		15	45	
West Byfleet Corner ...	7 45				
Byfleet ...	7 55	8 0			
Cobham (White Lion) ...	8 5	8 10			
Esher (Windsor Arms) ...	8 18				
Tolworth (Ewell Road) ...	8 25				
Malden (Cross Roads) ...	8 16	8 31			
Barnes (Railway Hotel) ...	8 31	8 46			
Hammersmith (Greyhound Motors) ...	8 38	8 53			
Oxford Circus ...	8 58	9 13			
London (Poland Street Coach Stn.) ...	9 3	9 18			

To WEST BYFLEET and GUILDFORD.

SUNDAYS.

		Then at minutes past each hour		
London (Poland Street Coach Stn.) dep.	a.m.			
Oxford Circus ...	9 8			
Hammersmith (Greyhound Motors) ...	9 28			
Barnes (Railway Hotel) ...	9 35			
Malden (Cross Roads) ...	9 56			
Tolworth (Ewell Road) ...	10 3			
Esher (Windsor Arms) ...	10 11			
Cobham (White Lion) ...				
Byfleet ...				
West Byfleet Corner ... arr.	10 21			
Ripley (Post Office) ... dep.				
Guildford (Horse & Groom) ... arr.	10 35			

FOR WOKING, ALIGHT AT WEST BYFLEET CORNER, THENCE BY "GENERAL COUNTRY SERVICES" BUS No. 36 or 37.

ADDLESTONE - NEWHAW - BYFLEET (When working)

Coaches leave Addlestone for Byfleet on Weekdays at 7.15, 7.45, 8.15, 8.45, 9.4, 9.34 a.m.
  ,,   ,,   Sundays   ,,   7.45, 8.15, 8.45, 9.15, 9.45, 10.15 a.m.

Coaches leave Byfleet for Addlestone Daily at 10.6, 10.36, 11.6, 11.36 p.m., 12.6, 12.36 a.m.
Minimum Fare :—Addlestone and Byfleet 1/-

FOR ADDITIONAL SERVICE BETWEEN GUILDFORD AND LONDON (Oxford Circus) SEE TIME TABLE FOR "SKYLARK" ROUTE BG.

The timetables of routes G (to Guildford) and Y (to West Byfleet Corner) as operated in October 1932. The apparently extraordinary amount of time allowed between Oxford Circus and Poland Street might be noted.

21

grounds that 'No service shall continue after 31 March 1931 which was not operating before 9 February 1931 – Road Traffic Act (1930) PSV (Transitory Provisions) (No 2) Order, 1931'. An extension of the Tring service to Aylesbury from 18 February was similarly disqualified, coaches returning to the Tring terminus on 1 April. These changes of timetable involved switching vehicles from Leavesden Road to Tring and back again, together with rewriting the entire schedule. A service between the Embankment and Upminster by way of Aldgate and Ilford was advertised to start on 25 February but did not in fact do so.

Had Green Line secured more vehicles before 9 February the services to Upminster via Barking and via Ilford would have had a secure legal base. However, to mount services at such speed made the events of January 1931 a remarkable month's activity which would have been even more noteworthy had it been possible to start two peripheral routes based on Guildford. These would have worked from Guildford to Dorking, Redhill, Sevenoaks and Dartford, and from Guildford to Woking, Windsor, Uxbridge, Rickmansworth, Watford and St Albans. Local licences were obtained but it was not feasible to go further. In the event, over 30 years were to pass before route 727 covered the Uxbridge to St Albans section of these proposals. For many years Green Line were to remain wedded to the concept of the route that travelled to, from or through Central London.

Top: T225, a front-entrance Regal, on Green Line route Z, licences for which were refused by the Traffic Commissioner and which therefore ran for the last time on 3 October 1933. The building operation in the background is an early stage in the construction of Windsor garage in St Leonards Road. *George Robbins Collection*

Below: T317 was an AEC Regal with Hall Lewis coachwork originally owned by East Surrey and transferred to Green Line in January 1932. It is shown at the Sunbury Common terminus. *George Robbins Collection*

4 Enquiry

It was clear from the outset that the official policy regarding coach operation would be a restrictive one, a point made by the Minister of Transport in December 1930 on the advice of the London and Home Counties Traffic Advisory Committee. Thus the proceedings of the Metropolitan Traffic Commissioner were to a degree pre-judged by Ministerial direction.

Green Line presented their 27 services (needing by this time some 275 vehicles) for licence, identification assisted by the first lettering scheme which was devised in February 1931. The letters chosen were usually the initial letters of the out-London destinations – for example, route C ran to Chertsey, G to Guildford – but there were exceptions in that X became the Westerham and Sevenoaks service and Z ran to Windsor via Slough. The route letters appeared on publicity material as it was reprinted and on the roof indicator boards rather later – these roof boards were to remain standard equipment on Green Line for over thirty years. The ultimate destination appeared on the front of the vehicle either under or above the 'Green Line' stencil (depending on whether one was looking at a member of the second or first series of T-type coach); initially through-London services did not indicate the final destination until the vehicles were quite near the central area – then the conductor changed the indicator at an appropriate point en route.

Green Line sought to reinstate the Tring to Aylesbury extension of route T and to restore the short-lived service from the Embankment to Upminster via Barking (route AV). Additionally, it was hoped to introduce a new service between the Embankment and Upminster, this time via Ilford (route AU). Application was made to run the coaches then terminating at Bushey through to Watford, whence they ran on garage journeys anyway. Route H – Harpenden to Great Bookham – was intended to run from Luton to Guildford, thus being extended at both ends. A new parallel service (AH) would have run from Dunstable to Guildford. It was hoped to extend the Rickmansworth service (P) to Amersham and Chesham and to put part of the Uxbridge service (Q) through to the same points via Gerrards Cross. Alternate Uxbridge coaches were to be extended to High Wycombe (AQ). Some coaches on route R – Reigate to Hitchin – were to work through to Baldock as AR and in the south the West Byfleet service (Y) was to be extended to Woking as route AG, making a closer association with the Guildford service. A new Y would have linked Woking, Weybridge and London.

The rulings of the Metropolitan Traffic Commissioner were made after protracted proceedings in which the operators who applied for licences

Harewood Avenue (near Marylebone Station), passengers for the centre being obliged to change to Underground, tram or bus.

There was further outcry – the coach operators created a skilled lobby and enlisted considerable public support. As a result the Minister set up a Committee of Enquiry on 30 January. Its membership included Lord Amulree (Chairman), Sir Hardman Lever and Sir Henry Maybury, the latter with long experience of London traffic problems through his work with the Advisory Committee. The terms of reference were to enquire into the operation of London Motor Coach services and the Committee began taking evidence in April. Frank Pick appeared on 19 April. He traced the origins of Green Line operations, including reference to the fact that the LGOC had long regarded suburban coach services (as run by independents in 1927 and 1928) as infringements of the 1924 Act. However, from the start made at Watford in October 1929, the LGOC through its operating agents had established a network of services that effectively covered the outer London area, and which were in vigorous competition with other services on almost every road.

Mr Pick gave his views on what he termed 'express omnibus services'. He thought a 30-minute service the minimum that would attract the travelling public; the minimum fare should be 1/- for the most part; stops should be fixed but not infrequent; peak hour traffic should be catered for by duplication rather than increased frequency of operation. His contention was that Green Line traffic was 40% business, 44% shopping and 16% evening travel for theatre and concert-going. In all, 65% of the passengers entered a circle within five miles of Charing Cross and 50% entered the central zone that the Traffic Commissioner had sought to ban to coaches. He felt it vital to bring the passenger as near to his destination as possible and believed that the termini suggested (The Elephant and Harewood Avenue) were impossibly inconvenient. He attacked the limitation of stopping places that had been recommended and cited the proposed Elephant to Dartford service that was allowed only six inter-

faced objections to almost every service from the railway companies and other operators as well. The scenes of confusion on the roads were thus transferred to the courts. Many applications were refused – Green Line would have lost over one third of their services had the first rulings been upheld – decisions that generated immediate appeals. A statement of policy by the Commissioner made on 5 January 1932 indicated clearly that he regarded coaches as supplementary to the railways, properly serving communities away from the railway lines. Further, he maintained that coaches should be excluded from a designated central area and terminated at the Elephant and Castle and

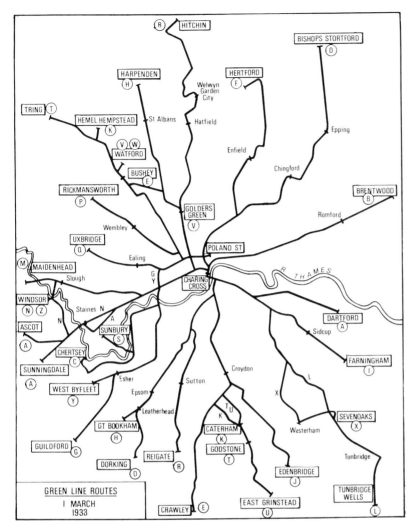

GREEN LINE ROUTES
1 MARCH
1933

Map labels:
HITCHIN (R) · HARPENDEN (H) · Welwyn Garden City · HERTFORD (F) · BISHOPS STORTFORD (D) · TRING (T) · HEMEL HEMPSTEAD (K) · St Albans · Hatfield · Epping · WATFORD (V)(W) · Enfield · BUSHEY (E) · Chingford · RICKMANSWORTH (P) · BRENTWOOD (B) · Wembley · GOLDERS GREEN (V) · Romford · UXBRIDGE (Q) · POLAND ST · Ealing · MAIDENHEAD (M) · Slough · G Y · CHARING CROSS · R THAMES · WINDSOR (N)(Z) · Staines N · A · N · DARTFORD (A) · ASCOT (A) · SUNBURY (S) · Sidcup · FARNINGHAM (I) · CHERTSEY (C) · SUNNINGDALE (A) · Esher · Croydon · L · WEST BYFLEET (Y) · Epsom · Sutton · X · Leatherhead · T U · SEVENOAKS (X) · GT BOOKHAM (H) · K · CATERHAM (K) · Westerham · GUILDFORD (G) · GODSTONE (T) · Tonbridge · DORKING (D) · REIGATE (R) · EDENBRIDGE (J) · TUNBRIDGE WELLS (L) · CRAWLEY (E) · EAST GRINSTEAD (U)

Below: A somewhat sombre-looking Blue Belle coach, a Regal, stands in a side road near Paddington. It ran to East Grinstead in competition with Green Line until the Blue Belle service was acquired on 20 July 1932. It was then designated AU. Interestingly, this route ran via Croydon Airport.
George Robbins Collection

mediate stopping places; the gap between Dartford, The Bull and Crayford Bridge was unnecessarily long. An appeal was made for stopping places about one mile apart, and the speaker suggested Gower Street and Portland Place as convenient Central London destinations. There was mention of the through route (the Hitchin to Reigate service was instanced) as a means of keeping coaches on the move through Central London and avoiding having parked coaches on the streets awaiting return journeys. Finally, Mr Pick stated that he believed that much of Green Line traffic was 'created traffic', derived from places such as the Kingston Bypass that had formerly been inadequately catered for.

Much other evidence was offered by other operators and objectors. After due deliberation, the Committee issued its Report on 18 June 1932. The Minister was recommended to restrict coaches from a defined central area and to demand that coach terminals should be provided off the streets. The Traffic Commissioner's suggestion of The Elephant and Harewood Avenue as turning points was supported, as was the proposal for stopping points about two miles apart. These findings clearly doomed Poland Street from the beginning – it was squarely inside the defined central zone – and it would have been impossible to continue the cross-London services already established. The majority of Green Line passengers who wished to travel somewhere near the centre would not have appreciated alighting from the coaches at the very periphery.

However, the operators, backed by public opinion, expressed great hostility to what they regarded as the negative quality of the Committee's findings and opposition, too, to the policy of the Traffic Commissioner which the Committee had upheld. In search of a compromise the Minister asked the Committee to reconvene and review the evidence placed before the Traffic Commissioner since the hearings began. In this second task the Committee showed a much more sympathetic attitude to the coach operators (and a better understanding of the needs of the travelling public). The Report, published on 2 August, reassessed the applications for licences so that many services previously disallowed were in fact permitted. Through routes were made possible by limited penetration of the central zone and the suggested stopping points were Oxford Circus, Portman Square, Trafalgar Square, Gillingham Street (Victoria) and Horse Guards Avenue. Also accepted was the need for stopping places no more than $1\frac{1}{2}$ miles apart in the area within five miles of Charing Cross, and more frequently thence to the edge of the Metropolitan Traffic Area. Outside this area coaches could stop at will.

Thus compromise was reached and it became possible to plan the future of the Green Line operation in the light of the constraints now identified. This task was to take over a year and the reorganisation was implemented on 4 October 1933 after a series of Ministry of Transport Orders. But meanwhile much was happening on the roads.

Right: A Leyland Tiger photographed on the short-lived service B to Beaconsfield which lasted only from 19 March 1931 to 14 October in the same year when it was cut back to Farnham Common. Premier was a vigorous competitor with Green Line and survived until compulsory purchase by the LPTB on 20 December 1933. *George Robbins Collection*

5 Development of the Green Line Empire, 1931-1933

For the most part, Green Line operations entered a period of stability so far as schedules were concerned after February 1931, many timetables then in use remaining unaltered in any detail until the reorganisation of 4 October 1933. Among the few alterations, services south of Chelsham were reduced to run every 120 minutes from 11 February 1931, and a revised series of timings was introduced on the Dartford services in the leaflet of 1 April when the coaches allocated to the routes were garaged at Crayford instead of Swanley. In 1932 a bus station was opened at Dorking on 16 March, and Hitchin coaches were rerouted via Stanborough Lane in Welwyn Garden City from 18 April. There were some alterations of frequency of operation on the Windsor and Brentwood services, and Leavesden Road garage was promoted to a coach station.

Green Line was in the process of establishing its corporate identity with the travelling public who were becoming familiar with – and remarkably loyal to – the coaches which were now in standard livery (all, that is, except the vehicles on loan to Amersham and District). The green uniforms of road staff also became immediate recognition features. Good publicity, a long-term concern of the LGOC, was directed to the interests of Green Line and the need for good public relations was impressed on all who had responsibility for the new services.

Having reached the limits of expansion allowed by the 1930 Road Traffic Act, further development of Green Line influence was possible only by acquisition of rivals' services. This became the policy and interest was shown as soon as competitors were granted licences. The first take-over occurred on 6 February 1932 when Green Line assumed control of the Skylark Motor Coach Company Ltd who had been granted licences to Hertford Heath, High Wycombe and Guildford.

This company had initiated a Guildford service on 23 December 1928, a service to Hertford on 16 November 1929 and had joined the two to work as a through route via Oxford Circus, every 60 minutes, on 1 December 1929. The High Wycombe route began on 14 September 1929. Green Line used the suffix 'A' for 'Associated' and coaches to Hertford Heath were allocated route letters AF, those to Guildford BG and to High Wycombe AQ. On 6 February also, Green Line secured the Regent Motor Service route running from Hertford to Oxford Circus approximately hourly; Safeway (A. W. Priest) had initiated this service on 26 August 1929. Financial negotiations for these take-overs often remained incomplete for some time, so that control by Green Line often preceded purchase of the undertaking. The original vehicles of companies – in the case of Skylark and Regent, these were Gilfords – remained in service on the routes, usually with large 'Green Line' stick-on labels on the sides. The maintenance of public goodwill – these services had built up considerable loyalty – was a matter of positive concern. The former Regent route became CF.

Bucks Express (Watford) Ltd, who ran every 15 to 30 minutes between their garage in Watford High Street (not the National establishment) and Oxford Circus, was the next acquisition made on 20 February 1932. This service had been started by Enterprise on 26 September 1929. Again, as in the case of Skylark, Green Line managed the service, as route AW, and issued the publicity until formal purchase was completed on 1 July 1933. The Associated Coaches (Ongar) Ltd service from Bishopsgate to Chingford and Ongar was secured on 31 March 1932. This service, begun by Lion Coaches Ltd on 15 February 1930, supplemented by the Curtis and Thompson coaches to Liverpool Street from Ongar, had settled down to run every 25 to 50 minutes in a slightly irregular

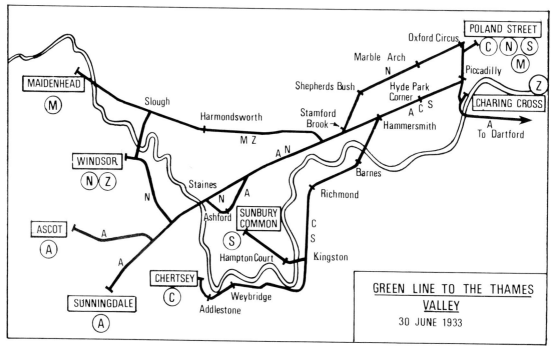

pattern; its coachworks were based at Bridge Garage, Ongar High Street. The route letters AO were allocated, and publicity was headed 'Green Line, formerly Associated Service.'

On 20 July the Blue Belle Motors Ltd service from Paddington to East Grinstead was acquired, a route inaugurated on 1 October 1930. Other services to Oxted and Westerham and to Caterham were not licensed. Coaches ran every 60 minutes via Godstone, Croydon Airport, Victoria and Marble Arch as route AU. Although relinquishing their suburban services, Blue Belle remained active between London and the coastal resorts and their half-deck coaches were familiar sights on main roads until the war.

Green Line secured a second route to Bishops Stortford on 21 September 1932 by gaining control of the Acme Pullman Services route from Charing Cross to Newmarket. Operations had begun on 5 October 1928 and coaches ran every 30 minutes to Bishops Stortford, less frequently beyond. This purchase was made by the LGOC and for some reason or other no route letter was ever allocated. The times to Newmarket were outside the Green Line sphere of interest and were sold to Varsity Express Motors.

The Red Rover Saloon Coaches route from Marble Arch to Aylesbury, dating from August 1928 and latterly providing 11 journeys via Brockley Hill and the Watford Bypass, was acquired on 29 November 1932. Green Line allocated the letters AT (to denote association with its own Tring service). Red Rover are still working bus routes in and around Aylesbury. The Kings Cross to Baldock hourly service operated by Queen Line Coaches Ltd passed to Green Line control on 27 April 1933 – this service had been started by Baldock Motor Transport Ltd in October 1928. This was the last take-over before the arrival of the LPTB on 1 July 1933, subsequent purchases being for the most part compulsory under the Act. Green Line thus added ten routes to its network in just over a year, together with premises at several points.

The formation of the London Passenger Transport Board brought Green Line a number of additional services and extensions of route. Drawing the boundary at Gravesend and Wrotham allowed the immediate extension on 1 July of A to Denton while the Farningham coaches (route I) ran through to Wrotham, The Square. The ACME purchase was finalised and 14 coaches were added to the coach fleet. Two routes added to Green Line were Oxford Circus to Hemel Hempstead (allo-

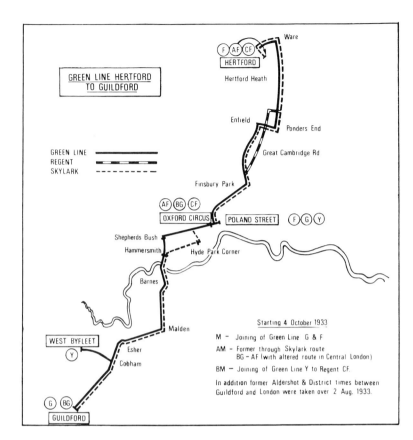

GREEN LINE HERTFORD
TO GUILDFORD

GREEN LINE ————
REGENT ════════
SKYLARK - - - - - -

Starting 4 October 1933

M – Joining of Green Line G & F

AM – Former through Skylark route
     BG – AF (with altered route in Central London)

BM – Joining of Green Line Y to Regent CF.

In addition former Aldershot & District times between
Guildford and London were taken over 2 Aug. 1933.

Below: An example of the poor facilities from which Green Line worked in the early days is shown in this view of the base at Ongar acquired from Associated Coaches (Ongar) Ltd in 1932. The coaches are allocated to route AO; three of them are second series T-types; the third from the left is a Reliance. *London Transport*

cated letters AF) and Charing Cross to Brookmans Park (BR). The Hemel Hempstead service, initiated on 22 September 1929 by West Herts Motor Services, ran every 90 minutes via the Watford Bypass and Abbots Langley. The Brookmans Park service was interesting in that its owner, C. W. B. Lewis of Potters Bar, seized on Cream Line as his title when he began running in September 1930. By the date of acquisition by LPTB five coaches, Gilfords, were being used. though only two passed to the Board. These last acquisitions came too late for them to be written into the Green Line scheme of 4 October 1933; on that date they retained their identities but were cut back to Portman Square. BR did not long survive the amputation.

The date of 4 October 1933 is an extremely significant one for Green Line as it marks the establishment of the network that, subject to changes of detail, became the basis for all subsequent operations. Except for a group of routes from Essex – Bishops Stortford, Ongar, Brentwood and Tilbury – which were turned in London, most services were operated as across-London journeys. Some links already established remained – Dartford remained loyal to Ascot and Sunningdale and the former Guildford to Hertford route still ran. For the most part, however, new connections were made and coaches from Tunbridge Wells ran through to Chertsey (C) or Woking (AC); East Grinstead saw departures for Harpenden (H) and Dunstable (AH); Chelsham routes were to Tring (E) and Hemel Hempstead (F). It will be noted that a new lettering scheme had been devised, basically on a clockwise system starting with Gravesend (A), Wrotham (B), Tunbridge Wells (C) and Sevenoaks via Westerham (D). The coaches, banned from the Central zone except for routes I and J, ran round it. Thus Gravesend to Ascot coaches travelled via Lambeth Bridge, Eccleston Bridge and Hyde Park Corner; Hertford to Guildford via Oxford Circus and Marble Arch. Coaches running through the West End on I and J were allowed to stop to pick up passengers in Regent Street after 19.30 Mondays to Fridays, 14.00 on Saturdays and all day on Sundays and Public Holidays. A similar restriction applied to

Left: A second series T-type coach unusually allocated to the former Regent service to Hertford. Although plainly Green Line and working with route letters CF, the former operator's title appears on the front indicator. Regent had used Gilford coaches. *George Robbins Collection*

Below: Still in the Cream Line livery, this Gilford served on the Lewis Charing Cross to Brookmans Park route until acquisition by the LPTB on 2 July 1933. The route was soon cut back to Portman Square where this view was taken on 16 July. Virtually the only changes are the BR route boards and the introduction of a two-man crew on a coach that seated 26 passengers. The service did not survive long enough to be written into the 4 October 1933 lists. *D. W. K. Jones*

Above: Tilbury Coaching Services (S. J. and I. M. Skinner) worked from Tilbury Docks to East Ham in competition with Batten's Coaches. Independence was retained until acquisition by the LPTB on 24 March 1934; the Grays and Tilbury Green Line operation was revised shortly after. *George Robbins Collection*

routes M, AM and BM when stopping outside Selfridges in Oxford Street. However, the fact that Oxford Circus was accessible to Green Line at all indicates how far the original proposal to ban the central zone to coach traffic had been modified. Poland Street Coach Station was closed – through routeing of coaches made it superfluous in any case. Control points for coach operation were thus established at Eccleston Bridge, Oxford Circus and Aldgate. An additional innovation on 4 October 1933 was, of course, the stopping limitations within the Metropolitan Traffic Area.

The services established on 4 October 1933 were derived from those of the original Green Line services allowed by the Metropolitan Traffic Commissioner, plus those allowed on appeal. To these must be added the ten routes taken over by Green Line between 6 February 1932 and 26 April 1933 and the two routes taken over by the LPTB on 1 July 1933. Within the constraints of the licensing system and because of the disapproval of Central London termini, the pattern of routes now mapped presented what was probably the best solution. A compromise was reached between what the travelling public wanted, what the authorities would allow, and what Green Line could provide. The long routes established by cross London working were more an operational necessity than a travelling amenity; relatively few passengers have ever undertaken journeys across the centre, though the importance of the facility that allowed them to do so should not be underestimated. Any long route must be more inflexible in its operation than a series of short ones, but Green Line was compelled to accept the disad-

vantages in its endeavours to make the best of the situation as it existed. There is no doubt that, once moulded into shape, the whole system tended to lose some of the attractiveness of the free-wheeling coaches in the early days of London services, especially in adaptability of operation and cheapness of fares. There was some loss of public loyalty as well, a feature of any amalgamation where individual units have won identity and goodwill. Rationalisation implies change and benefits to the system are not always seen as benefits to the individual traveller.

The LPTB Report of 1934/5 noted with some concern the results of the Amulree reorganisation. In the 12 months following 4 October 1933 the number of passengers carried by Green Line fell by 26%, the receipts fell by 24% while coach mileage had been reduced by only 9.5%. The usefulness of the coach services to the travelling public had been 'seriously affected' and Green Line represented 'a serious loss to the Board'. The coaches 'must now be subsidised from the earnings of other forms of transport.' The Board hoped for some relaxation of restrictions on routeing and stopping and looked for relief from 'onerous conditions' of operation. In fact, these ambitions were not achieved and the profitability of Green Line remained a matter of considerable concern until the war.

6 LPTB, 1933-1934

Whether or not Green Line management were concerned with the financial aspects of the operation, the policy remained expansionist. One new route to Gidea Park was inaugurated and operators still working limited stop coaches in the LPTB area were acquired. The fact that firms like Hillman and Premier had survived for so long and not submitted to approaches by Green Line during the first waves of acquisition suggests that they were financially secure and determined to maintain independence. However, the circumstances changed abruptly with the implementation of the London Transport Act.

Green Line opened Gidea Park to Aldgate and Horse Guards Avenue on 25 October 1933. The service, initially hourly to Romford, every 30 minutes from Romford to London, was intended to serve the large new housing estates on Eastern Avenue. The headway settled down to every 15 minutes, though the Aldgate to Horse Guards section was worked only during Monday to Friday evenings, on Saturday afternoons and all day Sundays and public holidays. The inauguration of this route represented considerable investment by the LPTB as 11 vehicles were allocated to it. It is

of note as the only coach route started by the Board.

Green Line acquired the East Ham to Aveley route operated by Price's Super Coaches on 1 December 1933, together with three coaches. Labelled AZ, Green Line maintained the service every 45 minutes, including the scheduled two garage journeys to Grays. The acquisition of the Aldgate to Grays and Tilbury service of the Amal-

Below: This Gilford 1680T coach, seating 31 passengers, was originally (and very recently) number 30 in the Strawhatter fleet. It appears to be working on route X, Aldgate to Gidea Park via Eastern Avenue, based on the North Street garage in Romford, coded RF. *George Robbins Collection*

Above right: TR24c was a former Premier Line Leyland Tiger now in Green Line livery after the transfer of the Windsor and Farnham Common services to the LPTB. The changed use of the destination indicators compared with Premier style is interesting. *George Robbins Collection*

Right: A good side view of the Leyland Tiger coach, this one acquired from Maidstone and District. These somewhat rugged and hard-riding vehicles operated A1 and A2 until replaced by the 10T10s in 1938. The lower-case c indicated a coach classification. *London Transport*

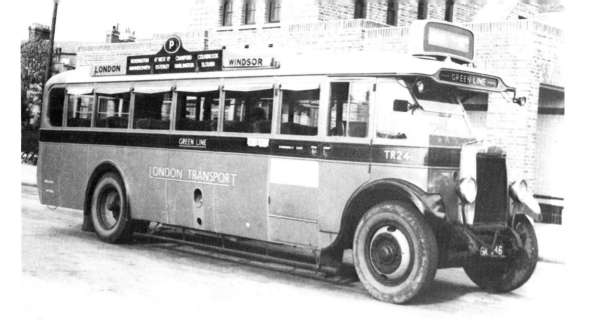

gamated Omnibus Services and Supplies Ltd (the coaches worked under the name Batten's Luxurious Coaches) on 23 December regularised what had been a long-standing arrangement. Batten's had been in association with Green Line from the beginning and vehicles had been made available; by the date of take-over London Transport had been handling the publicity for some time and were operating the service with ex-Premier vehicles 'On Hire to Batten's'. This became route Z and ran from Aldgate every 15/20 minutes to Grays, hourly to Tilbury.

The most significant gap in the Green Line map after 4 October 1933 had been on the Slough road;

the Green Line services M and Z to Maidenhead and Windsor had not been licensed and had therefore been withdrawn. However, this loss was recouped on 20 December 1933 by the take-over of the former Premier routes from Aldwych to Windsor and Farnham Common. These services dated from 27 January and 1 October 1930 respectively and were operated from a garage on the Bath Road in Slough, a characteristic iron structure incorporating a petrol station. Premier succeeded in getting licences for them, having lost their other services to Aylesbury, Beaconsfield and Sunbury. With vehicles surplus to requirements on their hands the company were possibly

ready for LPTB acquisition; 33 of them passed to Green Line. Four coaches hourly were operated to Windsor (route O), two to Farnham Common (P); O ran via Colnbrook Bypass, P via the village. Green Line timed these routes from Trafalgar Square, Cockspur Street.

A small-scale operation between Kingston and Ashford, dating from 1 July 1931 and running under the title Sunshine Saloon Coaches Ltd, was taken over by London Transport on 30 December 1933. This firm was associated with Bentalls, the department store; its title reflected some of the social values and optimism of the time – the great slump affected London and the south relatively little.

There was considerable change in the Romford area on 10 January 1934 through Green Line acquisition of the Aldgate to Upminster service, operated every five to 15 minutes by Upminster Services Ltd, and of the Bow to Brentwood section of Hillman's Saloon Coaches routes to Chelmsford and beyond. Hillman had been extremely active since beginning in November 1928 and his coaches reached far into East Anglia.

Sunset Pullman Coaches (not apparently related to the Sunshine Saloon firm in Kingston) were taken over on 25 January; thus a service that had been operating between Charing Cross and Brentwood since January 1930 came under the control of Green Line. These purchases allowed Green Line to reorganise route Y to Brentwood and AY to Upminster. Hillman surrendered 40 blue and white Gilford coaches to the LPTB, together with the large garage in Romford; Upminster Services supplied another 25 coaches and Sunset Pullman 13. LPTB purchases in the area were completed by securing the Fleet Coaches Ltd all-night service between Aldgate and Romford. One vehicle changed hands; the times were taken into the Y schedule but later (13 June) passed to Central buses. Green Line services to Brentwood and Upminster were always atypical, being in effect extremely frequent limited-stop bus services; they also ran extremely late at night and resumed very early in the morning. Doubtless they were profitable, passengers preferring road travel to the somewhat primitive facilities then provided by the LNER.

Above left: An early T-type coach on route V from Bishops Stortford pauses at Harlow one winter day in 1934. The shelter and the stop sign are relatively new. The reference to 1d fares indicates the bus fares available between Bishops Stortford and Epping, a facility that allowed the withdrawal of parallel bus services. *London Transport*

Above: The standard LPTB bus shelter shortly after its erection immediately opposite Hemel Hempstead garage at Two Waters in 1934. The interest the schoolboys are taking in the map is encouraging, though the ladies are taking a more detached view. *London Transport*

The purchase of West London Coaches brought an additional route under LPTB control on 17 January 1934. This was Victoria to Rickmansworth, Amersham and Aylesbury, with a connecting service to Chesham, dating from 19 May 1928. The operator, Mr Charles Holmes, apparently believed in variety and his fleet comprised three Saurers, two Daimlers, two Gilfords, two Tilling-Stevens and one Bean. Eight of these were acquired by London Transport and the route became route S.

A significant transfer to Green Line was the Strawhatter Kings Cross to Luton service on 1 February 1934. This was one of the first limited-stop services, starting in November 1927, and was initiated by Mr R. W. Priest (of Imperial Motor Services) who was active in several ventures north of London. There were several changes of owner-ship and of timetable, but by the time of the LPTB take-over coaches were running about every 30 minutes. Twenty-four coaches passed to Green Line who worked the route as BH; it retained its separate identity as late as 1950. The Strawhatter Motor Services garage became Luton South, coded LS.

Purchases on the Grays road were completed by the take-over of the Tilbury Coaching Services East Ham to Tilbury route on 24 March 1934. Four coaches were included in the deal. The following month, on April 27, the Kings Cross to Leighton Buzzard route (running via St Albans and Dunstable) was acquired; the operator, Beaumont-Safeway Coaches (W. D. Beaumont and R. W. Priest) sold three vehicles. The times were not worked by Green Line, Leighton Buzzard of course lying outside the LPTB area. Later that year, on 5 December, the Prince

Coaches service from Ongar and Chigwell to London passed into LPTB hands, together with eight coaches; similarly these times were abandoned as coach operations.

As a result of adding these services to the Green Line network, some route changes were made. The acquisition of the Sunshine Saloon service from Kingston to Ashford allowed the extension of D beyond Sunbury Common to Ashford and Staines, coaches running through from 31 January 1934.

There was considerable revision of services in the north-west consequent on the withdrawal of AF (Oxford Circus to Hemel Hempstead), AT (Marble Arch to Aylesbury via the Watford Bypass) and S (Marble Arch to Aylesbury via Rickmansworth) as separate operations on 10 July 1934. On the following day, coaches on route E travelled on from Tring to Aylesbury (every two hours on Mondays to Fridays, hourly at weekends). Similarly, route B was extended beyond Rickmansworth, coaches providing an hourly facility to Amersham, then running alternately to Chesham and Aylesbury via Wendover. Additionally route I was extended beyond Watford to Abbots Langley.

On 18 July route AZ (Grays to East Ham) was withdrawn as a separate working. From 19 September coaches on route H worked beyond Harpenden to and from Luton, and on 26 September routes A and AA were terminated at Gravesend Clock Tower, the short section between that point and Denton being abandoned by Green Line. These were relatively minor changes, largely matters of adjustment to the pattern of routes that had been established on 4 October 1933. This was really a period of consolidation, though there was still a lack of uniformity pleasing to the enthusiast who could travel on a wide range of vehicle types now running for Green Line, if not yet in Green Line colours. The backbone of the fleet was the T type coach, of two variants; some services however were operated by Leyland Tigers, others by several versions of Gilford. The identity of Green Line was not yet universally established in the London Transport area though steps to that end were becoming evident.

Below: A second series T shows off the lighter green livery adopted in November 1935. The small wooden boards at the back were additional features of this class; the ubiquitous Metropolitan Police Licence plate was standard to all stage carriage vehicles working in London at this time.
London Transport

7 LPTB, 1935-1939

The timetables established on 4 October 1933 had been devised on the standard time principle – ie on the basis that the same amount of time was allowed for a journey irrespective of the time of day. Thus an early morning or late evening departure was allowed the same time as a coach scheduled to run through the height of the rush hour (or the peak as the LPTB preferred to call it). However, changes in the Aldgate to Tilbury service starting on 5 June 1935 began the process of re-casting timetables so that additional time was allowed for peak-hour travel – usually six or seven minutes to London, 13 or 14 minutes on a through journey across London. An additional change initiated on 5 June was the abandonment of the prefixed letter A or B to denote a modification of the main route and the substitution of a numbered suffix. Diversion of some journeys via Aveley on the Grays road thus created Z2, Z1 being the original route. Alterations to existing route letters were made as timetables were revised and roof boards became due for painting.

An interesting acquisition occurred on 31 July 1935 when the long-established Redcar service – it dated from 16 September 1927 – fell into Green Line hands. Latterly, since 1 May, the hourly departures from Tunbridge Wells had been maintained by Maidstone and District; on and after 1 August they became Green Line which added five Leyland vehicles to its stock. The service continued to run alongside C and AC on its former timings until 7 January 1936. Then on 8 January the timetables were amalgamated and Tunbridge Wells was provided with a half-hourly service through the day every day on routes C1 to Chertsey and C2 to Woking. There were several other important changes made on 8 January including a reorganisation of services in Amersham. The coaches formerly terminating at Chesham were diverted to provide additional journeys on the main route B as far as Wendover; route R from London via Uxbridge was extended hourly to Chesham, in effect doubling the service to that town. Following the acquisition of the goodwill of the London to Horsham section of the Southdown Worthing service (formerly operated by Fairway Coaches), routes K and AK, now K1 and K2, were rearranged to include extension of K2 beyond Dorking to Horsham. This created the longest Green Line route ever, coaches taking four hours and 12 minutes for the through journey from Hitchin to Horsham. N was extended from Epping at weekends to Bishops Stortford thus providing hourly additional journeys over that road with the same bus fare table as route V (these had been introduced on 5 September 1934). There were alterations of detail to H and AH (now H1 and H2) and diversions of alternate journeys on T via Elstree were identified as T2.

All these service developments were incorporated in the first Green Line Coach Guide issued in February 1936. This well-arranged volume contained a great deal of introductory matter, mainly concerned with what to see in London and what to see in the country. There were time and fare tables for each route prefaced by a diagram which showed the stopping places in the Metropolitan area and bus and Underground connecting points. The appearance of this guide marked another stage forward in the creation of the Green Line image. A further stage was reached with the arrival of the 9T9 and Q-type coaches during the year which allowed the retirement of older vehicles, especially those like the Gilford machines acquired from former independent operators. The process of re-timing of services and changing of route designations went on during the year, the process ending on 29 July 1936 when BH became H3 and Luton to Kings Cross departures were increased to half-hourly throughout the day.

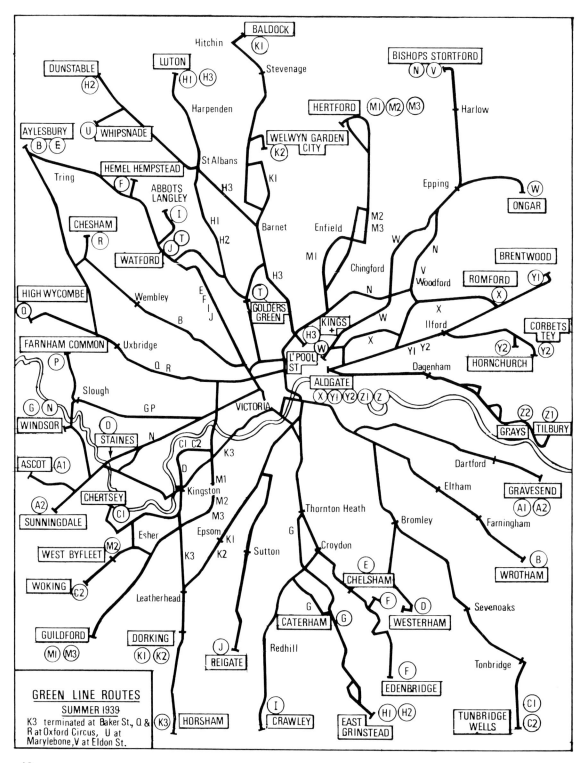

GREEN LINE ROUTES

SUMMER 1939

K3 terminated at Baker St., Q &
R at Oxford Circus, U at
Marylebone, V at Eldon St.

38

Shortly after this, on 19 August, route X was cut back to Romford, Gidea Park being served no longer by this route. Summer services to Windsor included for the first time a new Sunday route, Y3, which worked every 30 minutes from Brentwood to Windsor, coaches travelling from Aldgate to Trafalgar Square through what had been forbidden territory since 4 October 1933.

There were several developments during 1937 which were largely matters of rationalisation rather than service improvements such as had occurred during the previous year. Starting on 2 May 1937 A1 and A2 were diverted via Overcliffe in Gravesend following the opening of the new Northfleet garage. Route L (Uxbridge to Great Bookham) was withdrawn; additional journeys were provided between Oxford Circus and Ux-

bridge on routes Q and R, some of these on Saturdays and Sundays being extended to Gerrards Cross; this extension became a regular Summer facility. The London to Great Bookham section was covered by an extension of O from Windsor, every 30 minutes; alternate journeys on O were redesig-

Above: A first series T-type coach, T118, stands at Eccleston Bridge in December 1936 towards the end of its career as a Green Line. The rounded cab-front was characteristic LGOC design, seen also in the double-deck bus version. The limited accommodation at Victoria is evident; the Green Line travelling public is readily identifiable. *London Transport*

Below: The 9T9 coach was introduced to replace the first generation of Green Line vehicles. T452 loads at Eccleston Bridge on route K1 for Baldock on an August day in 1937. The Metropolitan Police plate still appears and the direction indicators are to be noted beneath the emergency door. *London Transport*

nated G and put through to Caterham via Hyde Park Corner, Piccadilly (stopping possible at restricted times of day) and Trafalgar Square. The 15 minutes service from Windsor via Slough was thus maintained, coaches running through alternately to Great Bookham (O) and Caterham (G).

In fact this arrangement of Windsor departures was further modified in the following year, though the diversion of Caterham coaches via Croydon Airport was maintained. Route P was altered to terminate at Horse Guards Avenue and extended beyond Farnham Common at weekends to Burnham Beeches. There were minor changes on the M services from Hertford, M1 now travelling via Turkey Street, M2 and M3 via Ponders End. The T2 workings via Elstree were withdrawn, all Golders Green to Watford coaches running as route T via Brockley Hill. At the end of the summer, together with the withdrawal of the special weekend facilities noted, routes V, X and Y1 from Bishops Stortford, Romford and Brentwood were withdrawn from the Horse Guards Avenue terminus, Aldgate becoming the furthest point of travel throughout the week. This change took place on 6 October.

Further route changes were implemented on 9 February 1938 when D was curtailed at Westerham, King's Arms, except for garage journeys to and from Dunton Green. After only eight months the Windsor via Slough services were again revised to operate as route G every 15 minutes to

Above left: The design of stop in 1937; there is a wealth of information clearly displayed. The ubiquitous LPTB shelter stands behind. *London Transport*

Left: An example of a free-standing information display board for country areas in 1937. The map is rather curious in that it is drawn on a projection that flattens the LPTB area. Subsequent maps have always emphasised the extent of the north to south distance. *London Transport*

Above right: A display outside St Albans garage in 1936. Enthusiasts welcomed news of Green Line Coach Guides, a very good two-penny worth. They were available from bookstalls and newsagents, but in practice conductors seldom seemed to carry them. *London Transport*

Right: The last acquisition by the LPTB for Green Line was of the former Redcar service from Tunbridge Wells which latterly had been operated by Maidstone and District. The times were passed to Green Line on 31 July 1935, together with five vehicles. This Leyland Tiger coach is at Horse Guards Avenue and in Maidstone and District livery; Green Line transfers are affixed. *D. W. K. Jones*

London, every 30 minutes to Caterham. Route O (Windsor to Great Bookham) was withdrawn, four journeys hourly between London and Leatherhead via Epsom being reduced to three by a reorganisation of the K routes. A new route, K3, Baker Street via Kingston, Hook and Chessington to Horsham (every 120 minutes, 60 at weekends) reduced the former long workings from Hitchin to manageable proportions. Great Bookham thus ceased to be on the Green Line map; it was never there, of course, on account of its own importance but because of its potential as a springboard for extension to Guildford. With the seasonal alter-

ations made at the beginnings and ends of summer the services remained largely unaltered except for matters of detail until the war. The 10T10 coaches appeared in 1938 and brought a significant improvement in comfort and performance, especially where they replaced the Leyland Tigers, and in 1939 the most advanced vehicles of their kind, the TFs, took over the services based on Romford and Grays.

The Green Line traveller in 1939 could read his coach Guide and find services and fares neatly detailed – the standard of presentation by Index Publishers, Dunstable, was excellent and never again attained. There was a map at the back of the book, but in addition the large free folded map issued by the LPTB was a useful supplement except when being used in the open air – it folded so as to provide a southern and a northern half and the act of locating the right half was rather complex. The line of route where stopping was restricted was marked in solid green line: otherwise two lines in parallel indicated where one could board or alight at will. At this time, of course, it was possible to ask the conductor to stop the coach (with one ring of the bell, but usually one tap of a pencil on the window behind the driver) anywhere to set one down, though in practice it took a bold traveller to ignore the conventional stops. He could take a single fare, minimum 3d in the country area 1/- in the Central area, or a return ticket that was available for a month – 'but not to make two journeys in the same direction; you

must go there and back'. Weekly and monthly tickets were available, starting on a Sunday morning. If the traveller lived in remote country he could ask for bus fares, the coaches carrying neat boards indicating '1d Fares on this Coach'. If he were a Londoner and found the queues rather long at his stop in the country he could return to London by train after 16.00 on Saturdays, Sundays and public holidays on payment of a supplement (a facility introduced 3 August 1935). Alternativ-

Left: For many years associated with the Guildford to Hertford routes, the 6Q6 introduced in 1936 proved a steady, reliable coach. The position of the engine can be clearly seen and the Park Royal plate is still in position under the driver's door. The radiator grill was partly cosmetic and partly an air intake. The 1d fares were available on coaches that ran via Hertford Heath. *London Transport*

Below left: Q205c is photographed at Marble Arch on its way to Guildford. The standard technique for negotiating this and other difficult corners is displayed: the semaphore arm is raised and the conductor points a warning hand. The driver of the van, however, appears entirely oblivious. *London Transport*

Above: A splendid line-up of 10T10 coaches at Hemel Hempstead (Two Waters) garage in 1938. They would appear to be newly arrived and equipped to take up service on routes E and F, although the letters visible on the roof boards of the first three coaches are incorrectly matched with the destinations shown on the blinds. *London Transport*

ely, of course, he could wait for a duplicate vehicle which on Bank Holidays might be a red Central bus; Tilling STs with their open staircases never quite looked the part working between Wrotham and Victoria.

The traveller would find services operating at least every 30 minutes except for route B (Wrotham to Aylesbury, basically every hour) and at the extremities like Edenbridge and Aylesbury which were offered coaches every two hours, Aylesbury by two routes. He could travel very early or very late; most last departures from Victoria were at about 23.30 – to Gravesend at 23.41, to Tunbridge Wells at 23.31. Last coaches arrived from London at Guildford at 01.16, at East Grinstead at 01.40,

and at Bishops Stortford at 01.53 (and then the coach had to return to Epping!).

The traveller might await his coach in one of the many green bus shelters to be found in the country area, whiling away his time looking at the map of coach and country bus routes that formed a centre piece behind glass. Hand raised, he would face the oncoming coach; the sliding door would be drawn back by the conductor – from experience it was almost impossible to open the door from the outside and in any case an attempt to do so was to deprive the conductor of one of his duties. Once inside the coach there would be an assessment of seating possibilities – or perhaps the option of standing if the coach were full and the conductor considered there were 'circumstances in which undue hardship would be caused if you were left behind'. There would follow payment of fare, sometimes after due consultation of the complex fareboard – and receipt of ticket: one ring of the Bell punch for a single, two for a return plus an attack by a hand clipper. The traveller would be able to see from his window a view of London and London's country that has now largely gone, except curiously for Epping and Sevenoaks which even today retain many visual characteristics of the 1930s.

The threat of war in 1938 had directed Government attention to the Green Line fleet and in June the Home Office in conjunction with London Transport devised a scheme of providing coaches with stretcher racks. After tests, the equipment was made and stored at garages. Announcements made on Thursday 31 August 1939 activated the plans and as coaches reached their garages the seats were removed and the stretcher racks inserted. Destination blinds were taken out and the word 'Ambulance' inserted; roof boards were removed and stored 'for the duration'. The coaches were then drafted to Central Bus garages and other strategic points where they awaited the bombardments that were expected to be mounted immediately on the outbreak of war, 3 September 1939. The whole operation was most carefully planned and executed, the only travellers inconvenienced being those whose weekly or monthly tickets had not expired, or those who had taken return tickets that could not be honoured. At the beginning of a war, however, these were minor considerations. London Transport's immediate concern was for the employment of Green Line crews, most of whom were eventually drafted to manning country buses; special problems arose, however, in such garages as Romford and Tunbridge Wells where there was little or no immediately available alternative work. Some bus services substituted for Green Line on and after 1 September, mainly over sections of route that had 1d fare stages; thus 396 ran from Epping to Bishops Stortford, 478 from Swanley to Wrotham. 'Service Suspended' labels appeared at Coach Stop signs, and Eccleston Bridge at Victoria became forlornly deserted. London awaited the war; Green Line represented an institution and an image that were no longer appropriate for the dark scene – it had literally vanished overnight.

Right: The interior of a 10T10, a pleasant and uncluttered environment in which to travel. Only the curved window winders and the decorative light and ventilator fittings in the ceiling betray the 1930s design characteristics of the Odeon and Gaumont cinemas. Very few of the clocks were extant when the coaches returned from wartime service. *London Transport*

Below: Three 10T10s on routes X, Y1 and Y2 stand at the recently opened Aldgate terminus in the spring of 1939. These coaches appeared on these routes for only a short period between 1938 and 1939 as they were replaced by the TF class when they were delivered. The Inspectors appear much more interested in the building work than in their coaches. *George Robbins Collection*

8 Wartime

It is a matter of history that the aerial onslaught on London, anticipated and prepared for on 3 September 1939, did not come. Government became concerned with the large number – over 400 – of Green Line coach ambulances that waited idly in depots; London Transport were concerned with acute problems of travel, especially in the east. Withdrawal of the routes from Aldgate to Romford, Brentwood, Corbets Tey and Hornchurch (Y1 and Y2) had left an embarrassing gap in travel provision and alternative facilities were both limited and inconvenient. Hence, an examination of the position in October 1939 allowed the re-start of Y1 from Brentwood to Aldgate, on and from 1 November; green STL double-deck vehicles were employed and worked a service that ran every 6–10 minutes from Aldgate to Romford, every 15–30 minutes beyond. In addition, Z1 and Z2 were re-started, providing a 15-minute service from Grays to Aldgate. The use of double-deck vehicles on these services was allowed by the Metropolitan Traffic Commissioner, permission dating from 1937 when London Transport made a blanket application for double-deck working on all Green Line routes that were not impeded by low bridges.

A further move towards normality, in what was a curiously abnormal situation, was the release of 153 coaches (9T9s and 10T10s) which allowed the restoration of route Y2 from Aldgate to Corbets Tey, coaches running every 6/10 minutes as far as Hornchurch, every 30 minutes beyond. This operation began on 13 December. A considerable improvement was thus effected in travel facilities in East London and Metropolitan Essex, an area at the time served otherwise by steam-operated suburban lines. There was undoubted passenger demand; as the 'phoney war' continued London recovered some of its confidence and resumed much of its business activity.

On 17 January 1940 routes A1 and A2 were restored, each on two-hourly basis; 10T10 coaches thus ran hourly between Gravesend and Virginia Water, every two hours to Ascot and Sunningdale. Compared with prewar the running times were slightly increased, a necessity for operating during hours of darkness when drivers had to follow the road in conditions of blackout with very limited – almost non-existent – headlight provision. On the same day, routes Q and R (Oxford Circus to High Wycombe and Chesham) were reinstated, each on an hourly basis though service beyond Amersham was limited to four journeys to Chesham. January 1940 was an extremely bleak month, with considerable ice and snow; the passenger numbers on these services could not have been very encouraging to Green Line. Two old-established services returned on 7 February: Luton and Hertford regained their Green Line links with London by the restoration of H1 (operated as H via Elstree) to Victoria and M1 to Oxford Circus and Shepherds Bush, respectively, each on a 30-minute headway.

A month later, on 13 March, H was put through to East Grinstead via Felbridge. Also, service was resumed on C1, Tunbridge Wells to Chertsey, coaches running every 30 minutes to Weybridge, every hour to Chertsey. The northern sections of E and F were reinstated on prewar frequency; coaches left Victoria hourly for Tring and Hemel Hempstead, those on E travelling beyond Tring to Aylesbury every two hours on Mondays to Fridays, hourly on Saturdays and Sundays.

Finally, in this wave of reinstatements, coaches began operating every 30 minutes from Portman Square to Epping on route N; on Saturday afternoons and Sundays the service was extended to Bishops Stortford.

To put Green Line developments in the perspective of history, route N was restored on 8

Left: Converted to an ambulance, T545 stands outside Westminster Hospital while patients are taken on board on Friday, 1 September 1939. The previous day the coach would have been on normal Green Line service.
London Transport

Below: A rear view of T612, also involved in the evacuation of Westminster Hospital on 1 September 1939. The nurse holds the patients' case notes. The sequence of photographs affixed to the emergency exit door indicate how stretchers should be loaded and off-loaded. *London Transport*

May. Two days later, on 10 May, Holland and Belgium were invaded and the rout of the West had begun. By the end of the month, the Dunkirk evacuation was in full flood, being completed on 4 June; Green Line coaches in ambulance guise were to be seen lined up outside London stations awaiting troop trains from the Channel ports. However, during this extremely uneasy summer the Green Line coaches ran on, still carrying Londoners to the Chilterns and to Sevenoaks; still carrying essentially business traffic from Gidea Park and Upminster. Increasingly menacing air attacks were beginning to reach London as the German air offensive intensified and a major day-light assault on 7 September caused great damage in the London Docks and the East End. (Against this background, it is perhaps not very significant to note the withdrawal of the Shepherds Bush to Oxford Circus section of M1 on 4 September). A night raid on 7 September was the forerunner of some 57 nightly visitations by bombing fleets that lasted to the end of 1940. Considerable disruption was caused to the life of London, and especially to communications. Railway services were halted by bomb damage on many occasions, main roads were blocked, tram tracks severed. It became increasingly difficult to maintain Green Line through routes and on and after 23 October

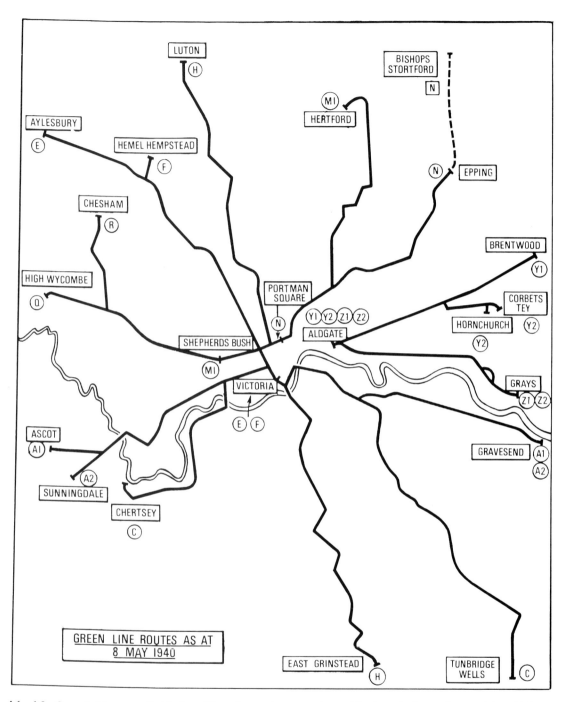

GREEN LINE ROUTES AS AT
8 MAY 1940

A1, A2, C and H were divided at Victoria, each section timetabled to run independently from that point. By this time the coaches – along with all London Transport buses and trams – were running with the windows obscured by thick net generously pasted on. A small aperture, diamond-shaped, was allowed in each pane, through which it was possible to see something of the current

Above left: Q210 heads a line of coaches converted to ambulances in a side road near Cricklewood garage early in the war. The regulation white paint on front wings proved difficult to apply to the 6Q6s, so it was applied where the wings ought to be. There was no such problem with the 10T10s further down the line. *D. W. K. Jones*

Centre left: TF69 and TF23, with EMS triangles on the front cabs, await duty outside Chalk Farm garage in the spring of 1940. They had seen only two or three months' service on Green Line before the threat of war brought about their conversion to ambulances. *D. W. K. Jones*

Below left: STL 2612 in appropriate Green Line livery is pictured at Aldgate on route Z1 soon after restoration of the service on 1 November 1939. The white paint on the wings is to be noted. STL 2612 survived to be transformed into an SRT in 1949 and was reallocated to the Central bus fleet. *George Robbins Collection*

Above: STLs 2619 and 1506 stand at Aldgate in November 1939. The vehicle on route Z2 has been painted in Green Line livery — it was formerly a red Central bus — but the Y1 is in Country bus livery; the front entrance of the second bus made it very draughty for passengers. The 'Out and About by Bus' posters are perhaps surprising, though the emphasis on fitness (through drinking Haliborange) was more in keeping with the time. *D. W. K. Jones*

devastation, even if frequent diversions took drivers and passengers along strange roads.

The need for speedy transport into and out of London became paramount and the Ministry of War Transport identified Green Line as the most effective agent available. Hence, priority was given to restoring those Green Line services that had not yet reappeared and a rapid programme of service development was planned in two phases, starting on 4 December and 18 December 1940. All services were to terminate at Aldgate, Victoria or Oxford Circus; all operated on regular time patterns and last departures from London were timed at about 19.30 As many routes as could be worked by double-deck vehicles were scheduled for them, and 180 STL buses were allocated from the Central fleet; finally the route letters were abandoned and replaced by numbers (for the first time in Green Line history), the numbers being selected so that a 'coach' could not be confused with a Central bus on the same road.

This programme called for initiative and organisation of a high order, especially in view of increasing staff difficulties and shortages, and the damage to vehicles caused by accidents and bombs. However, on 4 December services were restored to Wrotham (route 3), Redhill and Crawley (9), Reigate (10), Guildford (18), and to Aylesbury via Rickmansworth (35 – former route B), Luton via Barnet (46, former H3), and Bishops Stortford (53, former route V). All existing operations were re-scheduled and numbered; thus A1/A2 ran as route 2 from Gravesend to Victoria, being an STL assignment though occasionally Northfleet rostered an ST that lost time on Shooters Hill and Blackheath Hill. On 18 December, new services were put on to Dorking via Epsom (route 14) and Kingston (15), Staines via Kingston (allocated number 25 but actually operated as 21), Windsor via Slough (26), Farnham Common (26A), Hitchin (47) and Welwyn Garden City (47A). Also restored on this date was route X, now 54, between Aldgate and Romford via Eastern Avenue; the Y2 services operated as 58, though originally allocated the number 56. Aldgate had ample turning and

lay-over space; vehicles terminating at Oxford Circus were driven to Cavendish Square. At Victoria, the newly-opened Gillingham Street garage provided a valuable facility for vehicles and crews.

In the event, the operating problems for Green Line were probably at their worst during December 1940 as much of the day's work was undertaken after destructive night bombing attacks and in hours of darkness that tested driving skills and determination together. After the singularly vicious raid on the City of London on 29 December 1940, nights became quieter so that Green Line activity became more routine. Passenger loadings kept up well despite the gradual run-down of business in London and the shrinkage of purely pleasure travel that had provided much of the passenger clientele in pre-war days. Passengers carried in 1941 totalled 29,369,000; until closure in 1942 – 22,382,000. 1938/9 figures by comparison were 24,272,000.

There were very few changes in the timetable or organisation subsequent to 18 December 1940. There were one or two curiosities, including the

provision of paths for a 30-minute service from Watford to London that never materialised – gaps were left in the timetables of routes 40 and 40A to allow the operation of a 40B. Leavesden Road garage, a foremost Green Line centre before 1939, never again serviced a Green Line route. Aylesbury saw three coaches hourly from London, two via Tring (40) and one via Rickmansworth (35) – an over-provision, it seems likely. The Watford to Golders Green service was never restored, nor during the war were coaches to Woking, Westerham, Chelsham, Edenbridge, Tatsfield, Godstone, Dunstable, Ongar and Tilbury.

By 1942 world events were moving against coach operation generally and the Government, moved by the need to conserve fuel and rubber (in short supply since the loss of Malaya), decreed that coach services should be withdrawn in the autumn of 1942. Green Line services ceased on 29 September; the 'Service Suspended' notices were again brought out and Eccleston Bridge recaptured the forlorn look of September 1939. Vehicles and crews were readily absorbed into the Country fleet – passenger demand in the country area showing very significant increases during the war years. Garages solely concerned with Green Line operation were closed; Tunbridge Wells was used as a vehicle store and Romford, the former Hillman garage, became an aircraft component factory,

As to the vehicles, the Q and TF coaches remained as ambulances throughout the war – they were to be seen in and about London quite frequently on various routine missions. Some 9T9 and 10T10 coaches were retained as ambulances also, others were drafted into bus work; additionally 55 were allocated to the American Red Cross and were adapted to become 'Clubmobiles', 35 became USAAF personnel-carriers. They took to remote and unfamiliar roads, and 12 did not come back. As something of a balance, the Central STLs allocated to Green Line service in 1940 were permanently drafted to the Country fleet. And what happened to Green Line passengers? A survey undertaken by London Transport in April 1944 purported to show that 50% were not travelling – 20% were on Country buses, 10% on Central buses, under 10% on main-line railways; 10% had seemingly disappeared. This survey suggests either extreme loyalty to Green Line in that many passengers would not accept any other form of travel, or wishful thinking on the part of London Transport. Perhaps 1944 was a year in which it was difficult to find a representative sample.

While Green Line operations remained wholly suspended, consideration was given to the reintroduction of the system after the war. Forward plans were prepared at Reigate after Lord Ashfield gave Arthur Hawkins authority to make a start, his only stipulation being that the routes should be numbered and not lettered. As has been seen, the system of routes operating in 1939 had evolved from a number of services initiated by Green Line and other operators; the postwar plan was therefore formulated on a more rational basis than the competition that had triggered off the activity in the early 1930s.

During the planning stage, close liaison was maintained between the Reigate planning group and the Metropolitan Traffic Commissioner who ultimately had to authorise the routes, their timetables, stopping places and fares. Close cooperation was also established with the Metropolitan and

City Police authorities who gave advice on the roads to be followed, stopping places and termini. The principles established in the Amulree Report of 1932 were applied by the Traffic Commissioner and the Police, though there is no doubt that Green Line hoped to gain the access to the West End that had been a feature of the early years. Thus, the City Police were not prepared to allow coaches beyond Aldgate, except at weekends, and insisted that the former Eldon Street terminus at Liverpool Street should not be reinstated. This decision was of profound importance in shaping the routes to the east and north of London. All other routes had to be designed to operate as through routes, as in 1939, with Eccleston Bridge, Victoria as a central point. As will be seen, when the coaches returned to the roads, several services were terminated initially at Oxford Circus and Baker Street, in apparent contradiction of this stipulation.

With the plans for the new system laid, there was nothing more to do but await the end of the war.

Right: All Green Line coaches were withdrawn by Government direction for the second time on the night of 29 September 1942, and the stop signs were adorned with stick-on posters. The queue would have to wait until 1946 for the next coach. *London Transport*

9 Postwar Green Line, 1946-1950

The first postwar Green Line coaches began service on 6 February 1946. 9T9s and 10T10s were once again seen in London – as passenger-carrying vehicles rather than ambulances – on route 715 which linked Hertford and Guildford on a 30-minute headway. This was virtually a restoration of the prewar M1. On the same day the Bishops Stortford service was resumed, the London terminus now Aldgate. Coaches based at Epping ran under the number 720, with departures from each terminus every 30 minutes.

Clearly, much planning was necessary before even this modest start was possible. To begin with, vehicles had to be assembled and a programme of overhaul and refurbishing undertaken. Much of this work was done at Chiswick and a photograph published at the time showed a 9T9 resplendent in green livery and with new blinds alongside a similar vehicle bearing the grey paint and wartime insignia of the American Army. Additionally, staffing was a big consideration and although men and women were being demobilised in considerable numbers, they were not always available to staff garages where they were most needed.

The Metropolitan Traffic Commissioner would not agree to the operation of any express road services into London until 1 February 1946. This was to allow time for the restoration of stage carriage services to something near pre-war standards – especially in respect of evening travel. However the return of Green Line marked a stage in the rebuilding of London's travel facilities. So far as the public was concerned, 'Coach Stop' signs were restored, timetables appeared once more in place with red over-printing 'Starting 6 February 1946' and then the coaches appeared. Just before each route was restored, a modest advertising campaign was mounted in the London evening press and in appropriate local newspapers. As

there was an acute shortage of newsprint, the actual advertisements were quite small, but effective. Transport enthusiasts began to look out for them with cheerful anticipation.

On 27 February 1946 route 716 began operating hourly between Chertsey and Hitchin, two terminals that had not hitherto been associated. It was clear that the prewar system was not going to be the model on every occasion and that new patterns of service would be established. This feature of the restoration was made clear with the beginning of 704 on 6 March; this route ran every 30 minutes between Tunbridge Wells and Windsor and quickly acquired the reputation of something of a prestige service, probably a reflection of the kind of population it served. On the same date routes 709 and 710 began operations from Caterham and Crawley respectively to Baker Street; vehicles were allocated to Godstone and Crawley for these services. Route 723 began operation from Aldgate, every 20 minutes, to Grays, with one coach hourly running through to Tilbury Ferry. The last development of the 6 March phase was the start of the 721 which provided six coaches (actually STLs) hourly to Romford Market Place, and three to Brentwood.

There was another wave of activity on 3 April when 703 was inaugurated between Wrotham and Amersham on an hourly headway. This was a return of prewar route B, minus the Amersham, Wendover, Aylesbury section. 711 began Baker Street to Reigate, every 30 minutes; 718 linked Windsor and Epping via 1939 routes N and D, travelling through Central London via Fulham, Chelsea, Victoria, Marble Arch and Marylebone Road. 722 was opened between Aldgate and Corbets Tey on a 30-minute headway, though additional coaches – again, double-deck STLs – brought the service up to every 15 minutes as far

Above: T406 stands at Chiswick restored to its former pristine condition just before the resumption of the Hertford to Guildford service on 6 February 1946. Another vehicle of the 9T9 class, possibly T414 if the chalk marking on the front of the cab is to be believed, awaits attention after service with the United States Army. *London Transport*

as Upminster. Lastly Oxford Circus was linked to High Wycombe by an hourly service on route 724 (the prewar Q).

A further group of services began on 1 May. These were 708: East Grinstead to Hemel Hempstead and 714: Baker Street to Dorking via Kingston. These were both on a 30-minute headway. Route 717 was introduced to run between Woking and Welwyn Garden City, running for much of its journey over the route of the 716 introduced earlier and providing a combined 30-minute service. In addition, services on three routes were considerably augmented: 715 was increased to every 20 minutes; 718 and 724 to every 30 minutes. A measure of the extent of the task can be gauged by the fact that the developments on 1 May required the addition of 54 vehicles and something like 250 crew members; supporting engineering and clerical staff were also needed.

Four weeks later on 29 May route 705 began operations between Sevenoaks and Windsor via Westerham, thus supplementing 704 between Bromley and Windsor to provide a 15-minute service. 712 and 713 operated from Dorking via Epsom to Luton and Dunstable respectively, each service on an hourly headway. Finally, route 727 appeared as a virtually identical restoration of H3 running from Luton into the Coach Station at Kings Cross. Of special note in this group of restorations was the appearance of the yellow destination blinds which have been standard equipment of Green Line coaches ever since, though changed in design layout several times. On 19 June coaches began running hourly between Gravesend and Sunningdale on route 702 (the old A2); route 725 was inaugurated between Oxford Circus and Amersham (every 30 minutes), one coach hourly going on to Chesham. 701, Gravesend to Ascot, opened on 22 June (an unusual starting day in that it was not a Wednesday) to provide a half-hourly service with 702 as far as Virginia Water. Finally, routes 706 and 707 were to begin on 26 June to run from Aylesbury to Westerham and Oxted respectively, each on an hourly basis. Thus, together with the occasional route 726 to Whipsnade, which saw the first coach on 17 July, the postwar pattern was complete. It was a remarkably purposeful operation, not without operating problems of some significance; initially, vehicle allocations were sometimes mixed, though the 9T9s disappeared from coach work

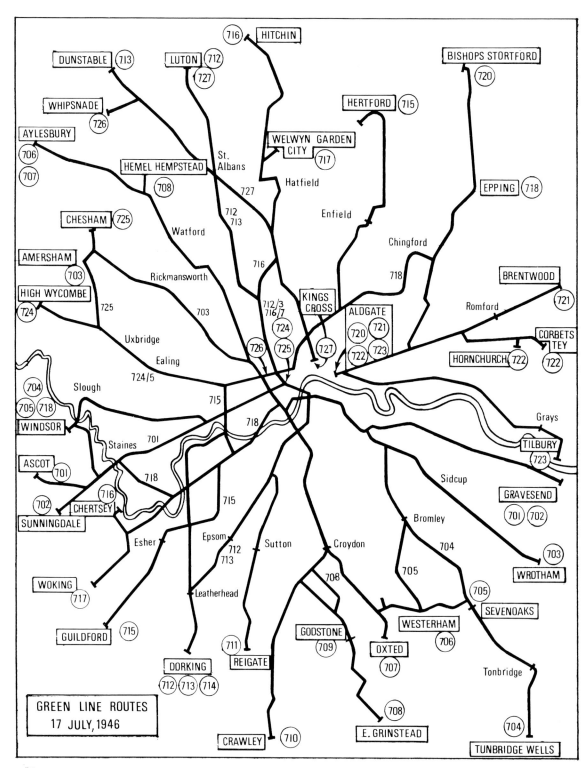

GREEN LINE ROUTES
17 JULY, 1946

54

Above: An entirely characteristic Green Line image is presented by T683 on its way up Polhill one evening in August 1947. At this time private motoring was extremely restricted by lack of petrol and the coaches often had the road to themselves.
London Transport

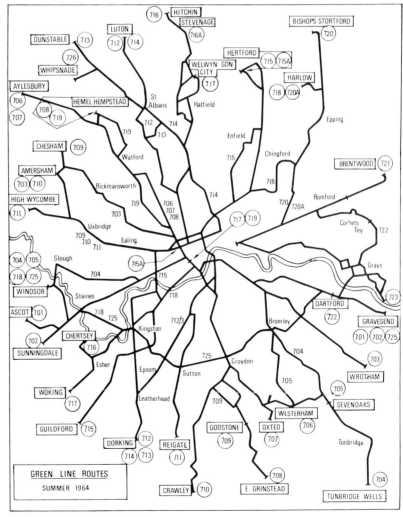

GREEN LINE ROUTES
SUMMER 1964

Above: Exemplifying the postwar livery adopted for Green Line, T684 has blinds and boards for the service to Whipsnade which was re-started on 17 July 1946.
London Transport

fairly soon. There was also the difficulty of route familiarisation for many drivers and this applied even to prewar crews who found themselves on new roads.

In comparing the immediate post-war map with that of 1939, it is apparent that there was some trimming of the extremities. Thus Edenbridge and Horsham remained unserved by Green Line; coaches no longer travelled to Farnham Common and 703 (the former B) was cut short at Amersham (leaving the section to Aylesbury to bus operation). Abbots Langley no longer appeared as a destination and Baldock remained off the map, coaches on the Great North Road turning at Hitchin. Another gap was the Epping to Ongar section of former route W; the Eastern Avenue route from Romford to Liverpool Street (X) was not reinstated. The London Passenger Transport Board Report for 1947 referred to 'a comprehensive system of routes' covering 'all the principal towns served before the war.' It was claimed that the system was 'a better coordinated one' and that withdrawals had been made where bus routes could effectively link up with the system.

In fact, the design and layout of the postwar routes were strongly influenced by the need to obtain efficient duty schedules. On the long through routes these were arranged to a standard pattern consisting of one round trip for each crew, a daily duty in the region of 7 hours 20 minutes together with a meal break of 40 minutes. The 30-minute headway was based on 32 return journeys on each route on weekdays, which formed 16 duties at each end of the route consisting of eight early and eight late turns. Where the length of the route made it impossible to work the standard duty pattern, shuttle crews were rostered to take the coach the last few miles of the journey and back, usually to the garage. The coaches were scheduled at the comparatively high speed of 18.38 miles per hour, each crew working on average 109.27 miles per duty.

Car miles travelled in the second half of 1946 were given as 430,000 per week, which may be compared with the 1938 figure of 530,000. There was thus a mileage drop of 20% but the number of passengers carried was very nearly the same. In terms of car miles, taking the 1933/4 figure as 100, then: 1938/9 = 104

    1947 = 83

Passengers carried in 1938/9 totalled 24,272,000; in 1947 the total had risen slightly to 25,281,000 – a rise of 4%. It may be noted at this point that Green Line, though 'firmly re-established as an integral part of the London Transport system' (LPTB Report) did not share the remarkable increase in activity noted in almost every other branch of public transport in the postwar years. Thus, the expansion of the Country buses can be judged from the following record of service car-miles operated:

	Central buses	Country buses	Coaches
1938/9	100	100	100
1946	95	152	57 (part-year only)
1947	100	154	79

Green line thus settled down to supply a steady and reliable service in the postwar period. There was some rationalisation of vehicles so that the Q type coaches were allocated to Amersham and High Wycombe for 724 and 725 and to Hertford and Guildford (for 715, formerly M1); TFs were stationed at Luton, St Albans and Dorking (for 712, 713 and 714), and at Grays (for 723). All other services were operated by the 10T10s except for 721 and 722 which were the preserve of double-deck vehicles. The STLs initially allocated to Romford were replaced by 37 square, somewhat primitive-looking basically wartime utility Daimler buses in full Green Line livery which made travelling an experience memorable by the somewhat hard ride provided.

There appears to have been some confusion of mind at 55 Broadway as to what market Green Line was supplying. The fare structure introduced post-war was not very encouraging. Initially, only single fares were available, at 1d per mile plus $16\frac{2}{3}\%$, later increased to 1d per mile plus $33\frac{1}{3}\%$. This brought a Green Line journey roughly to the levels of a railway monthly return fare, a charging system that did not offer Green Line any great advantage; a further problem was the coarseness of fare-stages. Thus, generally the first single fare in the range was 9d, the next 1/3 – at a time when 6d would purchase some five miles of bus travel. There seemed to be great fear of overwhelming existing services by encouraging travelling by cheap fares – hence Green Line was significantly under-used. There was some movement towards attracting passengers by the restoration of day return tickets from 1 October 1946, initially on Tuesdays, Wednesdays and Thursdays only and at restricted times. Weekly tickets had been made available from the previous day, ie 30 September 1946.

The period is remarkable, too, for the stability of the operation, perhaps even its rigidity. The only route changes were the joining of 709 and 710 from Caterham and Crawley to run through to Chesham and Amersham respectively (over former 725). Similarly, 711 was joined to 724 to provide a through service between Reigate and High Wycombe. The timetables remained standard so that it was possible to join coaches leaving Gravesend Clock Tower at 8 and 38 minutes past each hour, and Tunbridge Wells at 23 and 53. No attempt was made to differentiate times for peak-hour journeys as against off-peak so that there was some loss of accuracy of time-keeping according to the book – thus journeys on Sundays appeared very slow and early-running had to be guarded against. On the other hand, there was the great advantage from the travelling public viewpoint that services operated throughout the day at easily memorised times. At a time when London Transport, especially in the Central area, were operating a somewhat aged and miscellaneous fleet – including hired vehicles – Green Line presented a well-ordered appearance and was undoubtedly a well-crewed operation. Care was taken in the grooming of vehicles which were always well-maintained. In the case of the 10T10s the opening of the sliding door revealed a pleasing green decor, though most of the clocks fitted in 1938 had disappeared. The splendid ticket racks of prewar days were still a feature – conductors on long routes needed two, well-stocked racks with richly coloured tickets. A lasting mystery to the Green Line traveller was the conductor's preoccupation with his way-bill which needed a great deal of attention when recording sales of each price of ticket. The bell punch and the plier-clip remained standard pieces of equipment.

Of very considerable importance was the fares revision throughout the London Transport area in October 1950. For the first time travel costs were made the same whatever form of transport was selected; single fares on road services equated with day-return fares on British Rail and so far as Green Line was concerned the fare graduation steps were made much smaller. The result was to make Green Line the equivalent of the express bus and increasing use was made of the coaches over suburban and out-London roads: a valuable facility had at last been recognised. Green Line traffic which had fallen to 23,000,000 passengers in 1950 increased to 27,000,000 in 1951 (and to 30,000,000 in 1952) – a marked improvement in passenger use. Single

Above: An early postwar scene at Sevenoaks Bus Station, August 1947. T662 is in Green Line livery, about to take a 705 journey to Windsor, while T691 has been reduced to bus work and painted accordingly. The STL vehicle on service 402 retains its wartime white disc which aided visibility in the blackout. *London Transport*

Right: A new and very neat design at Marble Arch in May 1949. The pole has lost its rather fussy cap; the information is clearly and logically presented. *London Transport*

Below right: D170 was one of 37 vehicles in its class in Green Line colours allocated to Romford (RE) for services to Brentwood and Upminster. The austerity of the Duple body afforded few comforts. Appropriate for their time, they were replaced by RT type vehicles when these became available. *London Transport*

and weekly fares were available, return fares being issued no longer.

This phase of Green Line activity came to an end with the diversion of alternate journeys on 723 to run through Belhus Park Estate as 723A, this change dating from 4 July 1951. Subsequent major boundary changes in Grays in October brought other changes to 723 services, including later the provision of two journeys hourly to Tilbury, one running to Riverside, the other to the Civic Centre. The closing of the coach station at Judd Street, Kings Cross meant that 727 could no longer terminate there, thus ending a long association between Kings Cross and Luton dating back to Strawhatter days. On 30 September 714 from Dorking was extended northward to cover the former 727 road. These service changes and the arrival of the RF vehicles on 704 on 1 October mark the end of one stage of development and the beginning of another.

10 The RF Era, 1950-1962

The arrival of RF vehicles at Tunbridge Wells and Windsor and their starting service on 704 on 1 October 1951 marked the beginning of a period of over 11 years in which the RF coach was the standard Green Line, except of course for the RT vehicles allocated to Romford and Grays for 721, 722 and 723. Throughout these years the uniformity of Green Line operation was an essential characteristic and the identity of the service was assured; passenger numbers increased significantly (and at first steeeply) from 27 million in 1951 to reach a peak of 36 million in 1957, 1959 and 1960 – thereafter, the decline began. Passengers were assured of a standard product throughout this period whichever service they travelled on; increasing use brought positive management attitudes to development, and maintained good morale among crews. By comparison, Central buses had reached their peak much earlier – in 1951, Country buses in 1954 and 1955; the sustained popularity of Green Line suggests that the style of service offered was the positive preference of a new generation of travellers. Certainly, in engineering quality, appearance and standards of comfort the RF coach was in a class of its own; in all 263 were allocated to Green Line and delivery was completed by July 1952. Few would then have thought that some of these vehicles would be still in service a quarter of a century later.

A link with the past was broken in August 1953 when the Setright ticket machine was introduced in routes based at Romford; the machines rapidly became ubiquitous and the ponderous ticket racks were seen no more. The conductor's clerical work was much reduced – it became merely a matter of recording the total ticket register reading (the machine measured in half pence) at points en route. For the passenger, however, the neat green ticket was a poor substitute for the bell-punch multi-coloured tickets that had been a feature of Green Line accounting for so long.

The first development that occurred during this period was an interesting one – the provision of a service that was peripheral rather than diagonal. On 1 July 1953 Green Line opened route 725 on an hourly basis linking Gravesend and Windsor via Dartford, Bexley, Bromley, Croydon, Kingston and Staines. NF and ST were allocated four and three vehicles respectively and the service was a success from the outset, establishing a facility between places, for example Dartford and Bromley, that for many years had been almost inaccessible from each other by public transport. 10T10s were used as duplicate vehicles – the archway at Chislehurst being an obstacle to double deck use – and these turned at West Croydon. The

Below: A portrait shot of RF26 immediately before its introduction on 704 in October 1951. The wording of the upper line of the roof board is curiously spaced. London Airport was not entered by a Green Line coach on 704 until 1978, the appearance of the name on the board being somewhat misleading. *London Transport*

service was doubled in frequency between Dartford and Windsor on 28 April 1954, Dartford garage providing Green Line coaches (4) and crews for the first time since 1934. It was possible to travel on 10T10s which duplicated the service coaches well into 1955.

The next moves were in the direction of the new towns that by the mid-1950s were taking shape and seeking travel facilities. The first provision was of an hourly departure from Aldgate to Harlow New Town interspaced between the existing half-hourly coaches for Bishops Stortford. This service was designated 720A and provided a link for Harlow people who did not as yet have access to a railway station. The replacement of the RF allocation by 21 RT buses at Grays allowed for the additional service between Dartford and Windsor on 725 and the mounting of 720A. More vehicles were required for a radical reorganisation of routes 716 (Hitchin and Chertsey) and 717 (Welwyn Garden City and Woking) which was implemented on 5 October 1955. Basically the intention was to improve the service from Lemsford northwards to Stevenage, and by providing an additional route between Welwyn Garden City and London increasing services for the area to three per hour. 716 was thus supported by a 716A between Stevenage (White Lion) and Chertsey; 717 ran via Welham Green to Victoria. Of interest was the allocation of four RF vehicles to temporary accommodation at Stevenage, coded SV.

Further needs were identified and Green Line resources were tightly stretched. Hence, in April

1956 it was announced that 35 additional RFs would be allocated to the Green Line fleet — these were 19 former Country buses, six former Central buses and ten vehicles from the private hire fleet. All needed various adaptations before they were ready for Green Line service – the Central buses,

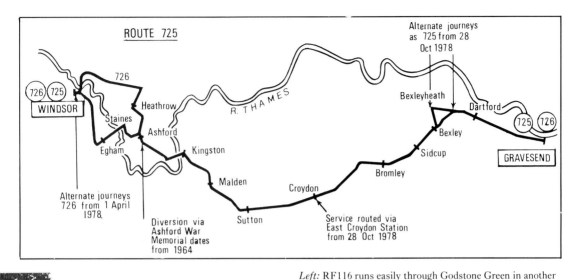

ROUTE 725

726 725
WINDSOR

Alternate journeys
as 725 from 28
Oct 1978

726

Heathrow

Staines

Ashford

Egham

Kingston

R. THAMES

Bexleyheath

Dartford

725 726

Bexley

GRAVESEND

Sidcup

Malden

Bromley

Croydon

Alternate journeys
726 from 1 April
1978.

Diversion via
Ashford War
Memorial dates
from 1964

Sutton

Service routed via
East Croydon Station
from 28 Oct 1978

Left: RF116 runs easily through Godstone Green in another characteristic Green Line situation in October 1954. Cars were still comparatively rare and looked antiquated compared with the coach. *London Transport*

for example, had to be fitted with doors – and on completion the whole RF series was renumbered, the coach allocation falling between 16 and 313. These additional coaches allowed the introduction of 719 between Hemel Hempstead and Victoria on an hourly headway; Abbots Langley was served once again, and between Stanmore and Cricklewood the road followed ran through Canons Park and Kingsbury. This service began on 11 July 1956, and on the same day route 718 (Windsor to Epping) was extended to Harlow Town Centre. With 720A three coaches per hour were now available between London and Harlow. An additional change, though one that did not require more vehicles, was the diversion of 712

and 713 between Borehamwood (Shenley Road) and Radlett in order to serve the new town area. Finally, on 8 August, route 715A was opened, coaches running hourly from Hertford, via the Heath, Ponders End and Edmonton to Marble Arch. The service supplemented existing 715 provision, though on different roads.

The impact of international affairs complicated matters for Green Line after the Suez fiasco of 1956. The supply of fuel oil became uncertain through the closure of the Suez Canal and from 17 December economies of operation were made. Thus services were reduced between Amersham and Chesham on route 709, between Dorking and Leatherhead and between St Albans and Luton on 712, between Chertsey and Addlestone on 716, between Epping and Harlow New Town on 718 and between Hornchurch and Corbets Tey on 722. Finally, 725 was trimmed at both ends, services being reduced between Gravesend and Dartford and between Staines and Windsor. When the political situation became clearer all these services were restored to full timetable on 1 April 1957. During the period of fuel restrictions, when private cars were less used, bus and coach operation generally enjoyed a bonus of passengers and

61

701 GRAVESEND - LONDON - ASCOT
702 GRAVESEND - LONDON - SUNNINGDALE

WEEKDAYS

GRAVESEND Clock Tower		6 8	6 38	8 38		9 8	9 38
Swanscombe George & Dragon		6 19	6 49	19 49		9 19	9 49
Dartford Market Street		6 31	7 1	31 1		9 31	10 1
Crayford Bridge		6 38	7 8	38 8		9 38	10 8
Bexleyheath Clock Tower		6 42	7 12	42 12		9 42	10 12
Welling Station Hotel		6 50	7 20	50 20		9 50	10 20
Shooters Hill Well Hall Road		6 57	7 27	57 27		9 57	10 27
Blackheath Green Man		7 5	7 35	5 35		10 5	10 35
New Cross Gate LT Garage		7 13	7 43	13 43		10 13	10 43
Old Kent Road Dun Cow		7 19	7 49	Then	19 49		10 19	10 49
Elephant & Castle St. Georges Road		7 24	7 54	at	24 54		10 24	10 54
Millbank Thames House		7 28	7 58	these	28 58		10 28	10 58
VICTORIA Eccleston Bridge		7 33	8 3	minutes	33 3	UNTIL	10 33	11 3
Hyde Park Corner Knightsbridge		7 37	8 7	past	37 7		10 37	11 7
Kensington High Street Argyll Road		7 44	8 14	each	44 14		10 44	11 14
Hammersmith Latymer Court		7 48	8 18	hour	48 18		10 48	11 18
Turnham Green Church		7 56	8 26		56 26		10 56	11 26
Brentford High Street, Fire Station		8 2	8 32		2 32		11 2	11 32
Hounslow Granada		8 12	8 42		12 42		11 12	11 42
Feltham Crown & Sceptre		8 18	8 48		18 48		11 18	11 48
Stanwell Bulldog	6 6 6 6 6 6	8 27	8 57		27 57		11 27	11 57
Staines Regal Cinema	6 15 6 45 6 49 7 11 7 49 8 11	8 34	9 4		34 4		11 34	12 4
Egham Eclipse	6 20 6 50 6 54 7 16 7 54 8 16	8 39	9 9		39 9		11 39	12 9
Virginia Water Wheatsheaf	7 9 7 22 8 8 22	8 45	9 15		45 15		11 45	12 15
SUNNINGDALE STATION	7 7	8 52		52		11 52	
ASCOT Horse & Groom	7 33	8 33	9 26		26		12 26	

G—From Staines LT Garage.

(TT.L1002)

704 WINDSOR - SLOUGH - LONDON - SEVENOAKS - TUNBRIDGE WELLS
Including journeys on Route 705 between Windsor and Sevenoaks via Westerham

WEEKDAYS / SUNDAY

	WEEKDAYS							SUNDAY	
WINDSOR Bus Station	5 53 6 8 6 23 6 38 6 53 7 8	23 38 53 8	9 23 9 38	6 53 7 8
Windsor Castle	5 56 6 11 6 26 6 41 6 56 7 11	26 41 56 11	9 26 9 41	6 56 7 11
Eton Burning Bush	5 59 6 14 6 29 6 44 6 59 7 14	29 44 59 14	9 29 9 44	6 59 7 14
Slough Crown	6 4 6 19 6 34 6 49 7 4 7 19	34 49 4 19	9 34 9 49	7 4 7 19
Colnbrook Plough	6 12 6 27 6 42 6 57 7 12 7 27	42 57 12 27	9 42 9 57	7 12 7 27
Bath Road Peggy Bedford	6 20 6 35 6 50 7 5 7 20 7 35	50 5 20 35	9 50 10 5	7 20 7 35
London Airport Three Magpies	6 23 6 38 6 53 7 8 7 23 7 38	53 8 23 38	9 53 10 8	7 23 7 38
Bath Road Travellers Friend	6 30 6 45 7 0 7 15 7 30 7 45	0 15 30 45	10 0 10 15	7 30 7 45
Osterley LT Station	6 37 6 52 7 7 7 22 7 37 7 52	7 22 37 52	10 7 10 22	7 37 7 52
Ealing Road Great West Road	6 43 6 58 7 13 7 28 7 43 7 58	13 28 43 58	10 13 10 28	7 43 7 58
Turnham Green Church	6 49 7 4 7 19 7 34 7 49 8 4	19 34 49 4	10 19 10 34	7 49 8 4
Hammersmith Latymer Court	6 57 7 12 7 27 7 42 7 57 8 12	27 42 57 12	10 27 10 42	7 57 8 12
Kensington High Street, Argyll Road	7 1 7 16 7 31 7 46 8 1 8 16	31 46 1 16	10 31 10 46	8 1 8 16
Hyde Park Corner Knightsbridge	7 8 7 23 7 38 7 53 8 8 8 23	38 53 8 23	10 38 10 53	8 8 8 23
VICTORIA Eccleston Bridge	7 12 7 27 7 42 7 57 8 12 8 27	42 57 12 27	10 42 10 57	8 12 8 27
Millbank Thames House	7 17 7 32 7 47 8 2 8 17 8 32	47 2 17 32	10 47 11 2	8 17 8 32
Lambeth Road Kennington Road	7 19 7 34 7 49 8 4 8 19 8 34	49 4 19 34	10 49 11 4	8 19 8 34
Elephant & Castle St. Georges Road	7 21 7 36 7 51 8 6 8 21 8 36	51 6 21 36	10 51 11 6	8 21 8 36
Old Kent Road Dun Cow	7 26 7 41 7 56 8 11 8 26 8 41	56 11 26 41	10 56 11 11	8 26 8 41
New Cross Gate Five Bells	7 32 7 47 8 2 8 17 8 32 8 47	2 17 32 47	11 2 11 17	8 32 8 47
Lewisham Duke of Cambridge	7 39 7 54 8 9 8 24 8 39 8 54	9 24 39 54	11 9 11 24	8 39 8 54
Catford St. Laurence Church	7 44 7 59 8 14 8 29 8 44 8 59	14 29 44 59	11 14 11 29	8 44 8 59
Downham Ashgrove Road	7 50 8 5 8 20 8 35 8 50 9 5	20 35 50 5	11 20 11 35	8 50 9 5
Bromley High Street, The Greyhound	7 54 8 9 8 24 8 39 8 54 9 9	24 39 54 9	11 24 11 39	8 54 9 9
Bromley Common The Crown	7 59 9 29	59 29	11 29 11 59	8 59
Farnborough (Kent) George and Dragon	8 8 A 8 38 A	8 38 A 8	11 38 A	9 8 A
Knockholt Station Approach	8 17 8 47	47 17	11 47	9 17
Pollhill Arms	8 23 8 53	53 23	11 53	9 23
Riverhead St. Marys Church	8 31 9 9 9 1 9 30 9 31 10 0	1 30 31 0	12 1 12 30	9 31 10 0
SEVENOAKS Bus Station	8 36 9 5 9 6 9 35 9 36 10 5	6 35 36 5	12 6 12 36	9 36 10 5
Tonbridge Station	8 58 9 28 9 58	28 58	12 28	9 58
Southborough Post Office	9 6 9 36 10 6	36 6	12 36	10 6
TUNBRIDGE WELLS Coach Station	9 12 9 42 10 12	42 12	12 42	10 12

A—Via Westerham (see Route 705).
For Faretable see page 47.
THEN AS WEEKDAYS
UNTIL
THEN AS WEEKDAYS (see Route 705). For Faretable see page 47.

(TT.1844/L494)

715 HERTFORD - ENFIELD - LONDON - GUILDFORD
715A HERTFORD - EDMONTON - LONDON Marble Arch

WEEKDAYS and SUNDAY

	SX SX SX SX SX SX									
HERTFORD Bus Station	5 40 6 0 6 20 6 26 6 40	7 0 7 20 7 26		40 0 20 26		9 26 9 40
Ware Grammar School	5 47 6 7 6 27 6 47 7 7	7 7 7 21		47 7 27 47		9 31 9 47
Hertford Heath Townshend Arms	6 31	7 31		31		9 31
Hoddesdon Clock Tower	5 56 6 16 6 36 6 39 6 56	7 16 7 36 7 39		56 16 36 39		9 39 9 56
Wormley Queens Head	6 3 6 23 6 43 6 46 7 3	7 23 7 43 7 46		3 23 43 46		9 46 10 3
Cheshunt Brookfield Lane	6 7 6 27 6 47 6 50 7 7	7 27 7 47 7 50	Then	7 27 47 50		9 50 10 7
Waltham Cross Queen Eleanor Stat.	6 13 6 33 6 53 6 56 7 13	7 33 7 53	at	13 33 53 56		9 56 10 13
Ponders End High Street, Technical Coll.	7 4	8 4	these	4		10 4
Edmonton Angel	7 11	8 11	minutes	11		10 11
Tottenham Seven Sisters Corner	7 21	8 21	past	21		10 21
Turkey Street Plough	6 18 6 38 6 58	7 18 7 38 7 58	each	18 38 58		10 18
Enfield Town Station	6 25 6 45 7 5	7 25 7 45 5	hour	25 45 5	UNTIL	10 25
Palmers Green Triangle	6 35 6 55 7 15	7 35 7 55 8 15		35 55 15		10 35
Wood Green Turnpike Lane	6 42 7 2 7 22	7 42 2 22		42 2 22		10 42
Finsbury Park Astoria Cinema	6 50 7 10 7 30 7 28	7 50 8 10 8 30 8 28		50 10 30 28		10 28 10 50
Camden Town LT Station	6 58 7 18 7 38 7 36	7 58 8 18 8 38 8 36		58 18 38 36		10 36 10 58
Oxford Circus Upper Regent Street	7 7 7 27 7 47 7 45	8 7 8 27 8 47 8 45		7 27 47 45		10 45 11 7
MARBLE ARCH Bayswater Road	7 13 7 33 7 53 7 51	8 13 8 33 8 51		13 33 53 51		10 51 11 13
Notting Hill Kensington Palace Gardens	7 18 7 38 7 58	8 18 8 38 8 58		18 38 58		11 18
Shepherds Bush Opposite LT Station	7 24 7 44 8 4	8 24 8 44 9 4		24 44 4		11 24
Hammersmith Butterwick for Broadway	7 28 7 48 8 8	8 28 8 48 9 8		28 48 8		11 28
Barnes Common Red Rover	7 35 7 55 8 15	8 35 8 55 9 15		35 55 15		11 35
Kingston Vale Robin Hood Gate	7 43 8 3 8 23	8 43 9 3 3		43 3 33		11 43
Malden Cross Roads	7 52 8 12 8 32	8 52 9 12 9 32		52 12 32		11 52
Hook Ace of Spades	8 0 8 20 8 40	9 0 9 20 40		0 20 40		12 0
Hinchley Wood Hotel	8 4 8 24 8 44	9 4 9 24 44		4 24 44		12 4
Esher Windsor Arms	8 8 8 28 8 48	9 8 9 28 48		8 28 48		12 8
Cobham White Lion	8 17 8 37 8 57	9 17 9 37 57		17 37 57		12 17
Ripley Post Office	8 28 8 48 9 8	9 28 9 48 10 8		28 48 8		12 28
Guildford Horse & Groom	8 43 9 3 9 23	9 43 10 3 10 23		43 3 23		12 43
GUILDFORD Onslow Street Bus Station	8 45 9 5 9 25	9 45 10 5 10 25		45 5 25		12 45

SX—Sunday excepted.

(TT.L1019).

Left: Three characteristic timetables from the winter 1958/59 Green Line Coach Guide. Route 715A had been introduced in 1956. Apart from this addition, these timetables were essentially those that had reopened the services in 1946.

Right: RF151 prepares to swing round Hyde Park Corner into Grosvenor Place on the 702 journey from Sunningdale. The style of destination blind is to be noted — it dated from 1946. *London Transport*

Below right: RF594, a Country Bus version of the RF type, waits to start a 718 Green Line journey to Windsor. Apart from lacking roof boards externally, the bus version did not have luggage racks inside — a quite serious deficiency when on coach duties. The forecourt is that of Epping garage; the date — 1955. *London Transport*

freedom from traffic congestion. Timekeeping was exemplary.

Progress was resumed on 12 June 1957 when 719 gained a half-hourly service (except on Monday to Friday evenings – the loss of evening traffic was beginning to be noticeable). On 25 July 710 was diverted to serve Gatwick Airport. Coaches began to appear with newly-designed roof boards; at first yellow lettering on a black background replaced the former gold on green; subsequently – and until the boards were finally abandoned – yellow boards appeared, the lettering in black. An unfortunate feature of 1958 was the seven week strike that halted all London Transport road services from 5 May until the resumption of 21 June. The dispute centred on payment for Country bus crews and the

compromise formula for Green Line drivers. There was considerable loss of goodwill (and passengers) on Central buses, but Green Line figures kept up remarkably well. On 15 October 1958 route 705 was diverted between Bromley and Keston to serve Hayes. In the following year new garages were opened at Hatfield (18 February) and Stevenage (Danestreet) (29 April). A slight thinning of 721 and 722 was implemented on 13 May. The winter of 1959/60 saw the reconstruction of Eccleston Bridge; coaches were sent over Elizabeth Bridge, and during the building work some new passenger waiting and queuing space was provided. The renewal was timely – the old accommodation had become extremely shabby.

With minor changes of timetable, the RFs went about their business. The summer of 1962 probably represented the peak of post-war Green Line provision; it also marked the end of a period of stability combined with steady development, as shown in the services to the New Towns. Daily vehicle requirement totalled 219 RF coaches and the 57 RT double-deck vehicles stationed at

Romford and Grays. Each garage operating RFs would hold at least one spare coach, and additionally two were held in Central London – one each at Riverside (R) and Gillingham Street (GM) to cover accident or breakdown. (They were in fact seldom used – a tribute to the skill of Green Line drivers and the sturdy qualities of the RFs). An analysis of departures from Eccleston Bridge on a Monday to Friday evening between 17.00 and 18.00 indicates 20 coaches leaving Westbound (for Windsor, Aylesbury, Ascot and other destinations), 13 Eastbound (for Gravesend, East Grinstead for example). Almost every one of these departures was duplicated either by provision of another RF vehicle or an RT in Green Line livery. The activity at Victoria was matched by that at Aldgate, 25 departures being listed in the peak hour – duplicate provision however being unusual on these services. Even so, there were indications that the passenger loadings were about to fall, as indeed they did – to 34,000,000 in 1961, and that the days of expansion were over.

Above left: A pleasing shot of RT3256, one of the 36 of its type serving from Romford (RE) during the 1950s. The route number in the canopy was illuminated all the time the vehicle was on the road. *London Transport*

Left: The Setright Ticket Machine revolutionised Green Line accounting in August 1953. It was first introduced on route 721. The immaculate appearance of the conductor is to be noted, as is the detail of the fare table. Ordinary return fares were available on this route, on 722 and on the Hitchin section of 716; they were an exceptional facility. *London Transport*

Below: A good example of London Transport information display, this board was photographed at Crawley Bus station in 1960. The Green Line map is to the fore, though the Southdown express coach facility is also advertised on the right-hand side. *London Transport*

11 Experiment and Decline, 1962-1969

The period 1962–1969 may be identified as one of unremitting decline. Certainly, passenger figures fell from 32 million in 1962 to 21 million in 1969, a sad commentary in itself. Many erstwhile Green Line travellers were doubtless driving their own cars; others possibly transferred to some revitalised railway services. As in all situations of diminishing numbers, some of the factors involved are outside the control of the transport operator, and the increasing road-use in London caused great congestion that delayed coaches intolerably. However, Green Line were in need of a new generation of vehicles by 1962 and the anticipation of double-deck operation by the Routemaster vehicles was perhaps untimely. In the event the fall in passengers carried revealed quickly that the larger vehicle was inappropriate, and as new single deck coaches were not available then some attempt was made to refurbish the RFs – still giving sterling service.

Towards the end of the decade, the London Transport Board (established 1963, following the demolition of the British Transport Commission) was itself overtaken by political decision that separated the Central Area from the Country Area; London Country, a National Bus firm, thus assumed responsibility for Green Line from 1 January 1970. Some of the decision-making with regard to Green Line assumes a somewhat ad hoc quality in the light of the impending change, and responses to falling traffic were often not more than temporary palliatives. However, there were promising initiatives taken – especially in the provision of two more peripheral routes – although the basic cross-London route remained the fundamental concept.

Following experiments with CRL4, the Routemaster Coach (RMC) duly appeared in August 1962, being allocated to the Hertford and Guildford garages for the 715 and 715A. The ambiguity of the publicity was immediately evident with the stress on the quality of the vehicle and the reduction of the main service to two coaches hourly (from three) in the timetable of 24 October. Admittedly, there was a loss of only three 'seats per hour', but that is not the way the traveller looks at a timetable which reduces his opportunities. 720 (Bishops Stortford to Aldgate), also equipped with RMCs, was similarly reduced from two coaches to one per hour. Allocation of the double-deck vehicles to 716, 716A, 718 and 719 was *not*, however, accompanied by reduction of service.

It would be tedious to catalogue the reductions in service and alterations to timetables in detail; almost every service was modified to some degree. Major withdrawals however are as follows: the Victoria to Rickmansworth and Amersham section of 703 (pre-war B) disappeared on the night of 3 November, 1964 – an early casualty, this, perhaps influenced by the success of the electrification of the Metropolitan line to Amersham. 722 from Corbets Tey to Aldgate, reduced to a Monday to Friday peak hour service only on 31 October 1965, disappeared altogether on 14 February 1969. The long-standing hourly service from Crawley was withdrawn on 22 November 1968, route 710 operating the following day between Baker Street and Amersham. The supplementary Hertford to London route via Hertford Heath, 715A, after several reductions, was withdrawn on 14 February 1969. On the same day the last journeys ran between Chelsham and Oxted and 707 disappeared from the working book as a separate operation. Finally, the long-lived 726 summer service to Whipsnade Zoo did not appear in 1969, being replaced by extensions of 712 and 713 journeys from St Albans. The Green Line map in 1969 was thus markedly different from that in 1962, although the reduced frequency of

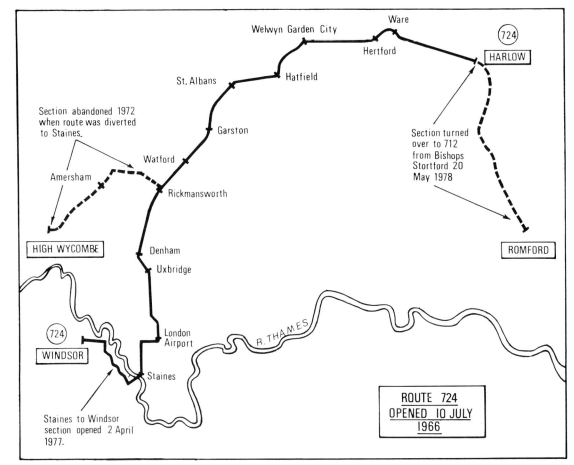

Welwyn Garden City

Ware

724

HARLOW

Hertford

St. Albans

Hatfield

Section abandoned 1972
when route was diverted
to Staines.

Garston

Section turned
over to 712
from Bishops
Stortford 20
May 1978

Watford

Amersham

Rickmansworth

HIGH WYCOMBE

Denham

ROMFORD

Uxbridge

724

R. THAMES

London
Airport

WINDSOR

Staines

ROUTE 724
OPENED 10 JULY
1966

Staines to Windsor
section opened 2 April
1977.

Left: RMC1503 at Turnpike Lane on its way to Guildford on
the Saturday variant of 715 serving Kingston. The RMCs
worked this route for nearly ten years from October 1962
until April 1972 when they were displaced by
one-man operated RP coaches. *Edward Shirras*

operation would not of course be apparent on it.

In what ways did Green Line take initiatives in
order to hold its position? We will look at some of
these in turn.

Provision of New Vehicles

The Routemaster coaches introduced in 1962
have already been noted. A further batch of
double-deck vehicles, longer than the originals
and designated RCL were put into service in
1965: 23 thus went to Romford for 721 (2 June)
and 722 (16 June). Seating 65 passengers, these
coaches represented a somewhat optimistic ap-
proach to these services that in the event was not
fulfilled. A further 14 RCLs were allocated to

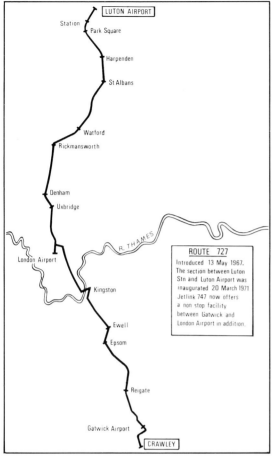

Above: Two RMC coaches, 1510 and 1492, stand at Hemel Hempstead Bus Station. Route 708 to East Grinstead was operated by these vehicles for the short period between 30 December 1967 and 15 February 1969 when they were replaced by one-man operated RFs. *Edward Shirras*

ROUTE 727

Introduced 13 May 1967. The section between Luton Stn and Luton Airport was inaugurated 20 March 1971 Jetlink 747 now offers a non stop facility between Gatwick and London Airport in addition.

Grays for the 723 services, but an awkward bridge at Thurrock prevented their use at first and they were exchanged with RMCs formerly working the 715 from Hertford. Some interesting 36ft-long coaches, Reliances, were drafted to Dunton Green and Windsor for operation of 705 from 28 November 1965. The 14 vehicles were in a new livery, basically light grey and green, the green in a broad band along the waist-line. The 49 passengers enjoyed panoramic views through 8ft-wide windows, the benefits of air suspension and force-air heating and ventilation. It was intended that these coaches should promote public discussion on vehicle policy for future Green Line operations, but unfortunately the RC class were beset with mechanical problems and were not very popular with their crews. Two years later they were replaced (by RCLs on 2 December 1967). They subsequently appeared

on other services in more standard livery – and hopefully in better order – most notably on the 727, of which more later.

Modernisation of Old Vehicles

The sturdiness of the RF coaches has been emphasised already, and a policy decision was taken to modernise them in 1965. By the end of 1966 70 had been rebuilt, the total reaching 175 by the end of the programme in 1967 (when the vehicles were already 16 years old!). Some were equipped for one-man operation, but apart from the new 724 (introduced on 10 July 1966) that was not possible until later. Certainly the refurbished coaches, with twin-headlamp sets and a broad green band along each side were externally pleasing; the interiors were cleverly re-styled. However, to undertake such work on an elderly set of vehicles was probably to store up trouble for the future, as London Country discovered in the end. The 175 re-styled RFs were exactly the right number to cover all London Transport Board single-deck Green Line operations in 1969.

Introduction of Express Operation

The intention here was presumably to make Green Line operations more attractive to the long-distance traveller. On 28 August 1963 route 705 was

Above: A very rare shot indeed — RT3246 emerges from the Dartford Tunnel on its way from Aldgate. RTs always looked well in Green Line livery. The extension to Dartford, initiated on 18 November 1963, was withdrawn less than a year later because of lack of patronage. *London Transport*

Right: The RF in bus form sometimes worked a Green Line roster. Here RF611 pulls away from the terminus in Wrotham, not far from the well-known Bull Hotel. After being provided with an hourly service since 1933, except of course for the war, Wrotham has seen only the peak-hour journeys on 729 since 31 March 1978. *Edward Shirras*

made to run 'Express' between Hyde Park Corner and Windsor via the Great West Road, Chiswick Flyover and Colnbrook Bypass. The scheduled time between these two points was exactly 60 minutes, compared with the 79 minutes taken by 704 coaches which kept to the conventional route. The only loss was that of the symmetry of the departures *from* Windsor; otherwise this was a promising experiment that probably paid off. The second express enterprise was a disaster. On 4 November 1964 route 709 was booked on week-days to run express between Amersham (LT garage) and Oxford Circus; coaches left the former route at Hillingdon and joined the A40 for a fast run via Northolt, Greenford and the White City. Unfortunately, the peak hour battle of the A40 roundabouts affected time-keeping badly, as did the daily congestion between Uxbridge and Denham. The express experiment in fact reduced the usefulness of the service and it was withdrawn altogether on 30 October 1965, having lasted less than a year. 709 thus shrank to Baker Street to Godstone only. 705 did rather better, surviving until 1 December 1967 when the coaches went back to the old style of running.

Bizarre Experiments

This may be an unfair judgement on the extending of 722 from Corbets Tey to Dartford through the newly-opened Dartford Tunnel on 18 November 1963. Coaches – actually RTs – worked every 30 minutes from Aldgate, hourly on Sundays, taking 97 minutes for a through journey. The final departure from Dartford was quite early, at 20.13. This was one of several bold attempts by London Transport which foundered on the fact that passengers were almost non-existent – the communities in Kent and Essex had been parted by the river for so long that no affinities existed as the basis for traffic flow. The extension to Dartford was withdrawn on 3 November 1964, having lasted less than 12 months. This severance proved almost

Above: The RF as modernised in 1966/67. This was something of a cosmetic exercise, though not unpleasing in result. The four headlights and the strips of chrome could not, however, disguise an essentially early 1950s vehicle at a time when other operators were introducing new designs. *London Transport*

Left: The modernised RF interior. The main changes were in the lighting fitments. The equipment for one-man operation is also evident. *London Transport*

Division of Through Services

the end of 722 which became a small peak-hour operation only from the following day, 4 November, which marked also the inauguration of route 727. This service was another 'Express working', this time between Tring and Victoria via Hemel Hempstead and Mill Hill. Part of the route was the M1 and coaches worked every hour on weekdays only. A revised timetable giving separate Monday to Friday and Saturday times was introduced, increasing the journey time from 91 to 97 minutes, but passengers were few. The service disappeared on 30 October 1965. It had probably been intended to capture some commuters dissatisfied with rail services during the electrification of the lines out of Euston, but in this it was conspicuously unsuccessful.

There were attempts to improve reliability of timekeeping by dividing through routes in London, changes which were introduced on 31 October 1965. Routes 701 and 702 were divided on Mondays to Fridays to run Gravesend to Hammersmith and Victoria to Ascot or Sunningdale. The overlapping between Victoria and Hammersmith certainly allowed passengers from Gravesend access to the Kensington shops, but that was exactly where major hold-ups regularly occurred – hence much of the potential of the experiment was lost. It was also a very expensive way to operate, increasing the service requirement by two vehicles, a point mitigated to some extent by turning early and late coaches from Gravesend at Victoria. The arrangement was thought sufficiently worthwhile to last until 17 May 1967; it never applied to weekend journeys which continued as through workings.

The second experiment was to divide 714 (Luton to Dorking) at Baker Street, the service to run in two separate sections on Mondays to Fridays. This does not appear to have been very worthwhile and the service returned to through working on 31 December 1966.

Exploitation of Peripheral Routes

Two interesting developments occurred in 1966 and 1967 when new traffic flows were identified on a peripheral basis rather than to and from the centre. It is perhaps curious that some 14 years should elapse since the initiation of the 725, a consistently successful service, before any parallel operations were implemented. However, on 10 July 1966 – a Sunday, an unusual starting day – route 724 was inaugurated to run from Romford to High Wycombe via Epping, Harlow, Ware, Hertford, Welwyn Garden City, Hatfield, St Albans, Watford and Amersham. Coaches ran every hour throughout the day, stopping only at 24 intermediate points – hence the 'Express' designation. An important innovation was the use of 'Pay as You Enter' coaches – the first on any Green Line service. The first timetable was clearly much too tight, being eased by 14 minutes on

Above: RF34 equipped for the 724 which began on 10 July 1966, the first Green Line service to be one-man operated. The additional 'Pay As You Enter' boards tend to clutter the vehicle. *London Transport*

Above right: Luton Station was the initial terminus for the 727 when the route started on 13 May 1967. RF99 appears to have been abandoned. *Edward Shirras*

Right: Eccleston Bridge became part of a one-way system in 1966 and the stands across the road fell out of use. RF168 is pictured on a 702 working, though deprived of its roof boards. *Edward Shirras*

7 August. The publicity emphasised the number of connections to be made at most stopping points. The second new service was the 727 which began on 13 May 1967, also one-man operated and an Express operation in that stopping points were limited. Coaches, modernised RF vehicles with luggage racks at the rear and Almex ticket machines, ran hourly from Luton station to Crawley, via St Albans, Watford, Uxbridge, Heathrow, Kingston, Reigate and Gatwick Airport. Again, publicity stressed the number of connections possible, especially by British Rail at Watford Junction. Equally important was the linking of Watford with London Airport – why had Green Line avoided the central terminal for so long? –

and with Gatwick. This was undoubtedly a well-planned service and it filled a number of gaps in the transport provision to and from the Airports, gaps which British Rail had been pressing London Transport to fill for some time. If such an exercise had been mounted in the early 1930s, doubtless it would have been identified with the names of A. H. Hawkins or A. W. Priest; in the organisational anonymity of the 1960s one wonders who it was who steered the project through the committee structure and had the satisfaction of seeing the coaches running.

Adoption of One-Man Operation

Green Line operations on a two-crew-member basis were clearly anachronistic by the middle-1960s; as the number of passengers fell the duties of the conductor became less and less arduous. Negotiations between London Transport and the Unions to remove him and to settle a pay award for the driver operator proved protracted; there was very proper Union objection to job loss, at the same time as it was difficult to provide crews for all services because of shortages of staff. However, agreements reached allowed one-man operation of 701 and 702, 719 (now extended to Wrotham), 710 (reduced to run hourly between Baker Street and Amersham), 711 and 714 – both

Above: RC1 took up duty on 705 from Dunton Green and Windsor in late 1965. The excellence of the passenger amenities — the coachwork was by Willowbrook — did not compensate for the mechanical problems to which this class was prone. *London Transport*

Above right: The second version of the Routemaster, as allocated to Romford and Grays — the RCL. Its additional length is indicated by the small windows built into the middle of the vehicle. The 65 seats provided became an embarrassingly large capacity in the late 1960s. *London Transport*

Right: RCL2258 awaits departure from Windsor. These double-deck vehicles replaced the flashy RC class and typified a very different operating idiom. *Edward Shirras*

reduced to hourly operations – and 720 on 23 November 1968. This change, essential in cutting the cost of service provision, was not without disadvantages to the passenger in that running times were extended (for example by 18 minutes on a through 701) and journeys were made tedious by the long periods that coaches stood at stops. A second batch of one-man operation was introduced on 15 February 1969 when 706, except for three Monday to Friday journeys from Westerham run as Chelsham to Aylesbury, 708 (formerly an RMC equipped route), 712, 713 and 725 were re-timetabled. The only conductors to be seen were those on double-deck vehicles and they survived until the London Country era.

Vigorous Fare Promotion

Green Line had always been very gentlemanly in its fare publicity, even reluctant to offer a bargain. It is true that limited day return fares had been experimented with in the 1950s and 1960s, but it was not until 6 June 1966 that 'Greenliners' became a standard part of the fares package. Even these were hedged about with restrictions – a journey could not begin before 09.30 on Mondays to Fridays and the return could not be made between 16.30 and 18.30. A more selective restriction would have been helpful – by the end of the 1960s there were empty seats on many departures during these times. An additional facility was the provision of a Golden Rover ticket which allowed unlimited travel on Country buses and Green Line coaches on the day of issue.

Perhaps not a matter of sales promotion but a useful facility nonetheless was the availability of bus fares over sections of Green Line route where parallel bus services had succumbed. Some routes had a daily bus fare structure, including Swanley to

Above: RAF displays at Biggin Hill have brought enhanced services on the 705, additional journeys being operated in the sixties by RT vehicles. RT640 is pulling away from a stop in Catford. The blind is not quite as well presented as it could be. *Edward Shirras*

Wrotham and Uxbridge to Gerrards Cross and Holtspur. On others the bus fare was a Sundays only feature, for example between Riverhead and Tonbridge and Hitchin and Welwyn Garden City. This had been a regular Green Line provision in the 1930s.

Thus Green Line operation in the 1960s was of considerable interest in that it was a period of innovation and experiment. Some of the initiatives would doubtless have been taken whether or not total traffic was in decline. Even so, the passenger figures in the last year of the London Transport period were not encouraging; what passed to London Country on 1 January 1970 was either a legacy or a liability, and London Country appeared ill-prepared to deal with either.

12 London Country, 1970 to date

Few companies can have begun operations in less promising circumstances than London Country Bus Services Ltd, which assumed control of the former Country area of London Transport. The sphere of responsibility stretched in a great arc from Tilbury round to Gravesend, with a Headquarters in Reigate. Literally the company had no centre: in form it pre-dated even the spheres of influence agreements reached between the LGOC, East Surrey and National. The boundaries drawn by the Greater London Council (as a traffic authority responsible for the newly-constituted London Transport Board) were, if anything, more clearly delineated than in the days of the LPTB. As a wholly-owned subsidiary of the National Bus Company London Country had to look outwards to Maidstone and District, Alder Valley or Eastern National in directions wholly inappropriate since 1933. London Country was thus an unwieldy empire, given independence by a powerful central state and not yet in a psychological position to align itself with neighbours beyond its own territory.

It had other problems too. It was equipped with vehicles of London Transport design and deprived of central facilities to maintain them. Also, they were past their prime – Green Line RFs were 19 years old when London Country inherited them; the newest vehicles – the RCs – dated from 1965 and were used in publicity material and Green Line leaflets as the latest coaches available. London Country became responsible for a rigid pattern of Green Line operation already obsolete except for the well-conceived peripheral routes. It began work in a period of accelerating decline in passenger numbers and remorselessly rising costs. When new vehicles became available, they were bought 'off the peg' and the Leyland National vehicles were mechanically unreliable. London Country has not had a good press; however, the management problems have been vast, and only recently has the measure been taken of them.

Thus Green Line settled into a spiral of decline in 1970, with falling traffic instigating reductions in service resulting in the loss of more passengers and good will. Trimming of timetables became a twice-yearly activity, and on 20 March 1971 710 – formerly running to Baker Street – was truncated to a short working, every 60 minutes, between Amersham and Uxbridge LT Station. The timetable as published encouraged passengers to buy day return tickets to London and to change onto the 711 coach in Uxbridge. An examination of these connections, however, reveals their ludicrous nature. A passenger taking the first coach on which such tickets were allowed would proceed as follows:

710	Amersham	dep	10.22
	Uxbridge	arr	10.58
711		dep	11.38
	Oxford Circus	arr	12.42

The return journey might start at 18.32 from Oxford Circus, include a 48 minute wait at Uxbridge and bring the weary traveller into Amersham at 20.56. It is unlikely that many day tickets were sold, not surprising that 710 had disappeared altogether by November 1972.

In the catalogue of withdrawals, most journeys on 712 and 713 terminated at St Albans on and after 29 May 1971, Dunstable being served by peak hour Monday to Friday and Sunday runs only. Most Westerham workings except those booked though to Chartwell disappeared from 706 on and after 1 April 1972, coaches running between Chelsham and Aylesbury as the main service. 702 to Sunningdale ceased operating on

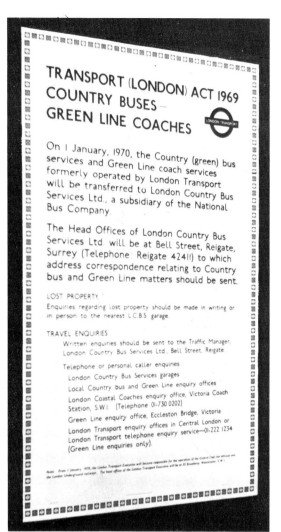

6 July 1973, the day the 723 was cut back to Grays from Tilbury. A further reduction in 712 and 713 confined the working between Victoria and St Albans after 31 May 1975, with a few Summer extensions to Whipsnade Zoo. The London to Dorking via Epsom section was maintained as 703 until withdrawal on 2 October 1975. Meanwhile, the long-established 701 (Gravesend to Ascot) was withdrawn throughout on 4 October 1975 – the loss of this service caused quite a public outcry, though not loud enough to make any difference. The Chertsey to Addlestone section of 716A was abandoned on 14 May 1976 coincident with reducing the 716 provision to an hourly service between Woking and Hitchin. Again, missed journeys had made the route notoriously unreliable.

Among the few glimmers of light in Green Line affairs, the 727 was extended to run to and from Luton Airport on 20 March 1971. The 724 (Romford to High Wycombe) was re-routed at Rickmansworth to parallel the 727 to London Airport and run thence to Staines. This was a logical development, only the few passengers wishing to travel to Amersham and High Wycombe being inconvenienced; for the first time since 1930 Amersham ceased to be on the Green Line map. The 720 was extended beyond Bishops Stortford to Stansted Airport on 4 May 1974, but this facility

Left: This poster tells its own story. For the first time since its inception Green Line had no link with 55 Broadway and headed for an uncertain future. *Edward Shirras*

Below: Fashions change too! Passengers wait to board RF89 at Crawley. The London Transport motif has disappeared from between the headlight sets. *Edward Shirras*

was provided at the expense of the timetable: clearly there was no possibility of allocating an additional vehicle to the service, so running times dictated the placing of the coaches 67 minutes apart. One wonders what A. H. Hawkins would have said about that.

Apart from schedule considerations, London Country had as a matter of urgency to end double-deck operation on Green Line routes – the RMC and RCL vehicles were almost embarrassingly large for the loads now carried. The programme began with the arrival of Reliance (RP) coaches for one-man operation on 721 on 1 January 1972; the RC coaches went a stage further in their chequered careers when allocated to Grays for 723 on the same date. Subsequent conversions to RP operation, all involving rewriting the time-tables though not significantly reducing services, were of 718 on 5 February, 716/A on 11 March, 704 and 705 on 25 March and 715/A on 29 April. The second priority was to replace the modernised RF vehicles. 725 received some new coaches, SMA class, originally ordered for South Wales, on 4 March 1972. The dreaded Leyland National vehicles duly appeared in 1972 and 1973; the LNB and LNC types allocated to Green Line marked the lowest point of coach provision; they incurred much criticism for their running charac-teristics and the austere quality of their furnishing. Travellers were not impressed by the plastic-covered seats; only with the arrival of SNC versions were some amends made with better seating and luggage racks. By that time, however, yet more Green Line passengers had made other travel arrangements. SNC vehicles were first allocated to 719 on 26 January 1974, the pro-gramme being completed with conversion of 711 on 4 November. Only at Chelsham were RFs regularly rostered as the longer modern coaches could not be housed in the garage. Another curiosity was the retention of double-deck working from Godstone on the peak hour 709 journeys – SNCs and one-man operation did not come until 15 May 1976.

Regrettably, vehicle allocation did not always achieve reality. In 1973 and 1974 maintenance problems were endemic. Both new and old coaches were off the road for long periods because of lack of spare parts, seemingly obtainable only after long delays. As a result, Green Line operations were often on an ad hoc basis, buses or coaches

being turned out for duty almost indiscriminately. For instance, for much of the summer of 1976 an RT with full blind display operated regularly on 706 and 708 – an astonishing feat for so elderly a vehicle. It has to be noted that London Country standards of vehicle care did not appear very impressive; chalked-in running numbers and inappropriate blinds were frequently seen. Vehicles were put on the road in deplorably unkempt states, often in seeming unreliable mechanical order.

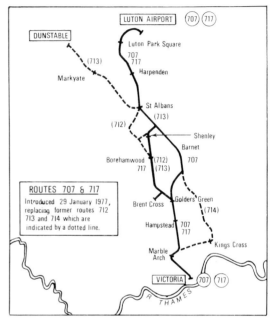

ROUTES 707 & 717
Introduced 29 January 1977, replacing former routes 712 713 and 714 which are indicated by a dotted line.

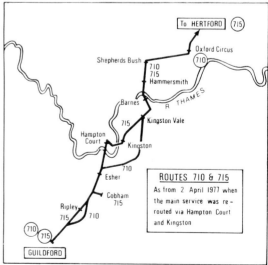

ROUTES 710 & 715
As from 2 April 1977 when the main service was re-routed via Hampton Court and Kingston

Additionally the policy of plastering the Leyland Nationals and other coaches with advertisements did nothing to enhance the Green Line image. One particularly horrendous sight was that of an RP in all-over advertisement form celebrating Wimpy Bars in 1976, while other coaches were used to advertise Embassy Cigarettes. Garages assumed the appearance of breakers' yards with discarded buses and coaches parked forlornly in spare lots. This must have been the most melancholy period in the history of public transport in any undertaking.

However, it would seem that London Country management began to take hold of the situation in 1976, at least so far as Green Line was concerned where missed journeys through staff or vehicle shortage had become commonplace. First, the new central maintenance base at Tinsley Green came into operation and vehicle reliability improved from that point. In addition, there was some energetic research into the kind of travelling facilities required by the public which led to identification of traffic flows and facilities. Much of the old Green Line system was doomed; the new developments, linked with the leasing of a new generation of Reliance vehicles bodied by Plaxton (RS) and Duple (RB), looks like retrieving something from the Green Line disaster. The first signs of the new and vigorously-pursued marketing policy came on 29 January 1977 with the opening of 707 (Victoria to Luton via Barnet) and its associated 717 (via Mill Hill, giving access to Brent Cross). Five RS coaches were allocated to St Albans for the service which took over much of the former 712/3/4 routes, though with fewer, shrewdly-selected stops. The introduction of these new services was accompanied by an effective publicity campaign and it was encouraging that

Left: In the last days of double-deck operation of the 718, RMC1472 is pictured leaving Windsor. The London Country 'Flying Polo' has been placed on the off-side rear panel. The route became one-man operated on 5 February 1972. *Edward Shirras*

Below: Seen leaving Amersham garage, RF172 works the remnant of 710. This short shuttle was clearly unsatisfactory; started on 20 March 1971 it lasted only 18 months. *Edward Shirras*

Above right: RF546 in early London Country unadorned bus livery works a 719 journey through Watford one overcast day in 1973. The vehicle is patently in poor shape. *Edward Shirras*

Right: SMA8 has just arrived at West Croydon on a short peak-hour working from Northfleet. This class spent almost all its time on 725 since initial allocation in 1972. *Edward Shirras*

there was public support for the additional journeys subsequently introduced. The southern section of 714 continued as an independent hourly operation between Dorking and Victoria.

The introduction of 702 (Bishops Stortford to Walthamstow) and 703 (to Waltham Cross) was based on sharpened perceptions of travel requirements and an exploitation of rail connections. These services, taking over from 718 and 720 (and bus routes 396/7) began on 2 April 1977 and quickly showed their usefulness in that the timetable was revised on 20 August, 703 being made a daily service – here grant aid from the

GLC was an important factor. The short, compact services were clearly more reliable in operating terms than the old routes they replaced, and the usefulness of the coach connections with British Rail (at Waltham Cross) and with LT's Victoria Line was stressed in publicity material. The former 718 was cut back to run from Victoria to Windsor, ceasing in the early evening; there is reason to believe it was intended as a summer service only, but it has so far continued on an all-the-year basis.

Also on 2 April 1977, Hertford to Guildford services on 715 were revised, coaches operating

hourly through Kingston and Hampton Court, and into and out of Cobham Village. Supplementary coaches between Hertford and Oxford Circus and between Kingston and Guildford afford a 30-minute service over these roads; on Saturdays a 30-minute service runs throughout. Two fast journeys from Guildford to Oxford Circus were scheduled as route 710, to run via the Kingston Bypass in the morning peak (returning in the evening) on Mondays to Fridays. Useful service though this undoubtedly is, the cutting of the 'normal service journey time to bring Central London within a mere 91 minutes direct from Guildford' might or might not appeal to seasoned travellers on Southern Region. An additional change on 2 April was the abandonment of the Croydon to Chelsham section; route 708 from this date worked hourly from Aylesbury to East Grinstead via Hemel Hempstead – a through journey of 4 hours 6 minutes. Finally, a useful development, 724 was extended beyond Staines to Windsor, providing a fast service via Runnymede and Datchet. Romford garage ceased to be responsible for this route, coaches and drivers moving to Harlow.

On 21 May, as part of the celebration of Jubilee Year, Green Line inaugurated a new, fast service from Victoria to Windsor. Operated hourly by RB coaches, journey time via the M4 was reduced to 54 minutes. Again, the new service was launched with appropriate publicity. The long-established 704 and 705 were routed into London Airport Central – a long overdue development. Additionally, on Sundays, at the insistence of Kent County Council as a condition of grant aid, some 704 journeys were sent through Knock-

holt Pound and Halstead. An interesting innovation was the diversion of alternate journeys on 725 after Ashford to run to London Airport Central and thence non-stop to Windsor. Without question, this diversion, numbered 726, has increased the usefulness of the service throughout 725 territory. Another significant change was the doubling of the 727 service between London Airport and Crawley, Reigate receiving an allocation of RB coaches for this provision. The focus of Green Line operation has thus shifted from Central London to Heathrow, a major change in Green Line thinking.

Amid all this development, the traditional routes continued to fail. 721 (Brentwood to Aldgate), reduced latterly to a 30-minute service, ceased altogether on 1 July 1977, Romford garage being closed. 711 (High Wycombe to Reigate) closed on 4 November, though some effort was made to replace this by a new route 790 running six journeys (seven at weekends) between Amersham, High Wycombe and Victoria. High Wycombe garage was subsequently closed.

Adjustments to services continued unabated in 1978, the year beginning with a sensibly revised version of 716. From 14 January an hourly service was booked to run from Hitchin to Victoria as 722 and 732, the latter operating number being used for coaches running on weekdays via Brent Cross. The publicity referred to 'Green Line's unique understanding of the travel needs of people in Hitchin, Stevenage, Welwyn Garden City and Potters Bar'. The new facility served fewer stops, provided a faster service and served Oxford Street. As part of the 'continuing improvement to the Green Line

Above left: Just arrived from Harlow, RP39 stands alongside the Wimpy Bar Green Line coach. 718 was reduced to Victoria/Windsor only on 2 April 1977 and is currently worked by RB or RS coaches. *Edward Shirras*

Above: A close-up view of RP46 at Windsor in full Wimpy livery. Placing this vehicle on the dignified Sevenoaks road suggests some insensitivity on the part of London Country. *Edward Shirras*

network', 716 was reduced to run hourly from Woking to Oxford Circus, its timetable appearing alongside 714 (Dorking to Victoria) and providing a joint 30-minute service between Kingston and Hyde Park Corner. Coaches were advertised to serve 'the Royal Albert Hall, and for lovers of rock music, the Odeon at Hammersmith'. Clearly, a new type of passenger was hoped for.

The next series of changes were involved with the withdrawal of 719 between Victoria and Wrotham on 31 March. This service had a long record of late running and unreliability, the subject of periodical outbursts in the local press. From the following day there was an interesting provision over this road. The long established Maidstone and District coach service from Tenterden to Victoria was converted to a limited stop coach operation of the Green Line type with the driver taking the fares. Five journeys were offered on weekdays, four on Sundays and the final picking-up point in the London direction was made Swanley Junction. Additionally, Green Line 729 came into being on 3 April as a Monday to Friday only operation affording one coach to Victoria in the morning peak and a return journey in the evening. A point of interest is that the service, worked by Swanley garage, is operated into the Maidstone and District garage at Borough

Green. For Brands Hatch travel Green Line reserved the number 739 for an express service operated on race days only. It would appear logical, given the relationship of London Country with Maidstone and District, to make all coaches on the Wrotham road a 919 activity, but doubtless problems of grant aid, licensing and union agreement did not let this happen.

In consequence of these alterations 719 was altered to run from Hemel Hempstead to Victoria and then on to East Grinstead, the former 708 (Aylesbury to East Grinstead) being cut back to Victoria. This was without doubt a change for the better – the former 708 was difficult to operate reliably because of its length, and the projection of 719 southwards made a neat matching with 709 which continued its peak hour working.

From Saturday, 20 May route 724 was shortened to run from Harlow to Windsor, the section of route between Harlow and Romford being taken over by new route 712 from Bishops Stortford. Route 703 thus disappeared, though bus route 329 continued the service to Waltham Cross. This revision in effect confirmed the success of the reorganisation of services in Harlow and Epping of the previous year. Changes from the same date, however, marked the disappearance of 705 as a regular daily operation, thus halving the provision to Sevenoaks and ending Westerham to London services altogether except on Sundays. 704 continued as the normal hourly stopping service between Tunbridge Wells and Windsor, supplemented by new route 701 from Victoria to Windsor via Hammersmith and the M4; after calling at London Airport coaches continue via Colnbrook, Langley and Slough, some going on to the

Safari Park. With 700, the non-stop service, three coaches hourly were provided in this timetable between London and Windsor. Sunday services became very complicated, with 704 running every 120 minutes from Tunbridge Wells to Windsor and 705 running – also every 120 minutes – between the same points but via Westerham. One Westerham working each way was

operated via Chartwell. To add to the complexity, the diversions via Halstead on 704 were maintained, and short workings on 705 were timetabled every two hours between Sevenoaks and Bromley North Station.

The final major change in Green Line operation during the year came on 28 October with the diversion of 725/6 in Croydon to run via East Croydon Station – a very important interchange point. Additionally, 725 was rerouted via Bexleyheath, adding five minutes to the running time but affording another very useful link.

Changes and developments in 1979 began with a reappraisal of the services based on Harlow. From 31 March the 702 (Bishops Stortford to Walthamstow) timings were confirmed, but part of the 712 service to Romford was diverted via Chigwell and Hainault and given the number 713.

Left: Newly-delivered Leyland Nationals were allocated to Green Line to prove themselves. This is an SNB, new at Hemel Hempstead, on a 708 London journey in April 1979. The rather spartan interiors of the bus version proved unattractive to Green Line travellers. *Edward Shirras*

Below left: The coach version of the Leyland National provided the Green Line traveller with improved decor and better seating. SNC151 has just arrived at Hemel Hempstead Bus Station. The London Country policy of disfiguring their coaches with advertisements is to be noted. *Edward Shirras*

Below: A sign of better times was the arrival of the RB and RS coaches. RB69 is seen leaving Windsor on its non-stop leg to Heathrow on 726 in April 1979. The London Country bus stop sign is attached to a former London Transport post. *Edward Shirras*

712 and 713 were also routed via The Wake Arms. A major change to an old-established route occurred on 28 April when the 704 was severed at Eccleston Bridge. From that date services from Victoria to Windsor thus comprised the non-stop 700 (introduced for the summer), a sharply timed 701 and the standard working on 704; a fourth coach hourly, of course, works via Kingston on 718. A revised timetable was provided for Tunbridge Wells to Victoria, now numbered 706 and incorporating the eccentric 705 pattern on Sundays. Much longer layover periods at Victoria should facilitate more reliable running than in the past.

An innovation of great promise came on 28 April with the initiation of a non-stop service between Gatwick and Heathrow on the appropriately numbered Jetlink 747. Five coaches in special livery were allocated to Staines for working this route. Departures from each terminus are booked hourly, the journey time being 'approximately 70 minutes'. The attractive leaflet announcing the service included a plastic timetable sheet doubtless intended for the wallets and handbags of jet-age travellers, a new generation of occupants of Green Line seats. More traditional customers were provided for by the diversion of four journeys each way on Sundays on 716 to run from Addlestone to Staines Station via Thorpe Leisure Park; this new working began on 1 July.

Another service at the planning stage is an orbital route from Staines via Heathrow to Ealing, Wembley, Brent Cross and Wood Green. This would be provided by diverting one departure per hour from Hertford which would take the

Above: RS15 pauses at Brent Cross one day in April 1979 on its way from Victoria to Luton Airport (route 717). Vehicles of this type have brought some respectability back to Green Line. *Edward Shirras*

number 734; 735 would be the new Hertford to Oxford Circus route, 715 being confined to London to Guildford journeys. If implemented, this series of changes would mark the end of one of the longest-lasting cross-London services.

It is evident that Green Line operation now falls into several clearly-defined categories. First, there is the last of the traditional cross-London routes, 715 (Guildford to Hertford), now under threat, and the last of the Aldgate services, that to Grays on 723, which struggles on. Next come the survivals of the old services. These include the 706 (formerly 704) from Tunbridge Wells to Victoria and the remnant of the 704 from there to Windsor, though usefully diverted into London Airport; the 719 from Hemel Hempstead to East Grinstead, an amalgamation of parts of former 719 and 708; the 714 and 716 from London to Dorking and Woking respectively, remnants of much longer through-London workings; 708, now running from Aylesbury via Hemel Hempstead to Victoria; the 718 between Victoria and Windsor via Kingston; and the vestigial remain of 709, confined for some years to peak hour and Sunday journeys from Godstone to Baker Street. Then comes a group of ambitiously re-vamped services; these include: 707/717 providing an hourly service between Luton Airport and Victoria, the 722/732 from Hitchin to Victoria, 701 from Windsor to Victoria running fast between Hammersmith, Butterwick and Heathrow, and 790 offering a two-hourly coach from Amersham to

Victoria, via High Wycombe. Non-stop express operations comprise the summer Victoria/Windsor service, the 700, and the newly introduced Jetlink 747. There is also the limited stop operation between Guildford and Oxford Circus, the peak hour 710.

Peripheral routes include the original 725 (Gravesend to Windsor), the only one of this group *not* to serve London Airport; 726 between the same termini diverts at Ashford and runs into Heathrow Central. 724 and 727 (Harlow to Windsor and Luton Airport to Crawley respectively) are rather faster routes with fewer stops.

At the other end of the scale are the 'local' Green Line routes based on Harlow, the 702 from Bishops Stortford to Walthamstow and the 712/713 to Romford. The timetable for these routes refers to 'Bus' and, significantly, they are the only daily routes now scheduled for RP coaches. Mention must also be made of the peak-hour workings between Borough Green, Wrotham and Victoria on 729; 709 already referred to could be included in this category. In addition, 737 runs on Sundays and public holidays to Whipsnade, the 739 on race days to Brands Hatch.

In addition to all this activity, Green Line now appear on summer coastal services, running on licences transferred from National Travel. These include daily services from Gravesend to Bognor Regis and from Croydon to Walton-on-the-Naze. The writer recently encountered a Green Line coach on the road from Colchester to Clacton-on-Sea, and the following day saw another speeding through Aldershot. He has not yet become used to seeing Green Line out of its natural context, but doubtless will adjust his thinking in due time.

13 Green Line on the Road: Coach operations in Sevenoaks and Romford

Sevenoaks, just 22 miles from Central London, has managed to preserve its identity through the years and though its population has increased from 17,500 in the 1930s to 22,000 in 1971 it has maintained its coherence as an urban unit (to use planners' jargon). It is an attractive town, with pleasing streets and good shops. It has Knole Park and Knole House as two impressive places to visit and is also a good starting point for explorations of the beauty of the nearby Downs, Ide Hill, Toys Hill and Bayley's Hill being especially rewarding. It is perhaps the most characteristic town of a number south of London, including East Grinstead, Reigate and Dorking, that are staging points on the roads to coastal destinations and which have avoided the worst perils of ribbon development. Coherence and identity are important and when one is in Sevenoaks one cannot possibly make the mistake of being anywhere else.

Sevenoaks was squarely in East Surrey territory, the garage at Dunton Green being opened in 1922. It was (and is) served by Maidstone and District Services to the east, and by Autocar from Tunbridge Wells. A small local firm, West Kent, was also active in routes to local villages and via Ide Hill to Edenbridge. It was the Autocar rival, Redcar, however, that took initiative in providing a limited-stop coach facility; they began a pre-booking service from Tunbridge Wells on 16 September 1927. From the London direction Glenton began a Victoria to Sevenoaks service the same month; six journeys were provided each way on a pre-booking basis. Neither of these ventures appeared very secure as the Glenton operation was withdrawn in December, the Redcar service suspended on 1 January 1928. However, Redcar revived on 5 April 1928 and began running without the pre-booking condition. The next experiment was by Safeway, the A. W. Priest interest, who instituted five journeys from London to

Sevenoaks in June 1929; interestingly, the coaches were booked to run through from Reading in June 1930, though the extension proved fatally weakening and the whole operation was withdrawn two months later. Finally, Anne Coaches of Dorset Street, Sevenoaks put on four journeys daily from Sevenoaks to Victoria via Farningham on 1 March 1930, but this venture was also unsuccessful and lasted only a few months.

Autocar entered the field as an agent of East Surrey on 6 June 1930 with an hourly departure from Tunbridge Wells to Oxford Circus, a half-hourly service operating from 24 June. Sevenoaks thus had the benefit of the Redcar and the Autocar services. East Surrey coaches reached the town in their own right on 18 October 1930 when their Oxford Circus to Westerham route was extended to run hourly to and from the White Hart. The Autocar and East Surrey services were routed into Poland Street on 28 January 1931, the Tunbridge Wells service leaflet now headed 'Green Line operated by Autocar'; in due time the standard red and black of the LGOC coaches operated by Autocar and East Surrey gave way to the coach colours of Green Line. The services advertised in 1931 were maintained until the 1933 reorganisation, except that the coaches travelling via Westerham were started at The Chequers. On 4 October 1933, the following services came into existence:

C   Tunbridge Wells (Limehill Road) to Chertsey (The Bell) hourly
AC   Tunbridge Wells to Woking (hourly from Sevenoaks on Mondays to Fridays, hourly from Tunbridge Wells at weekends).
D   Sevenoaks to Sunbury Common via Westerham (hourly).

Three coaches per hour were thus available to London, with an additional hourly departure by

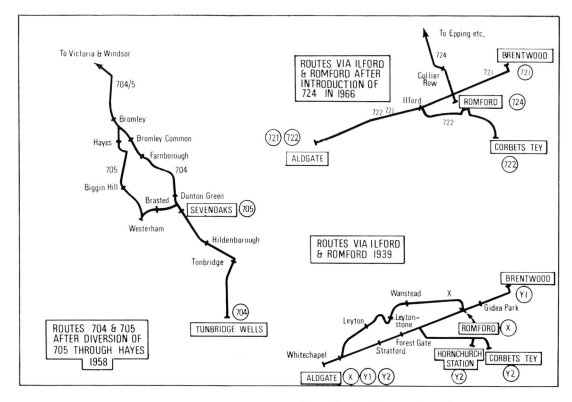

ROUTES VIA ILFORD
& ROMFORD AFTER
INTRODUCTION OF
724 IN 1966

To Epping etc.

BRENTWOOD

724

Collier
Row

Ilford

ROMFORD 724

721

721

722 721

722

721 722

ALDGATE

CORBETS TEY

722

To Victoria & Windsor

704/5

Bromley

Bromley Common

Hayes

Farnborough

705

704

Biggin Hill

Dunton Green

Brasted

SEVENOAKS 705

Westerham

Hildenborough

Tonbridge

ROUTES VIA ILFORD
& ROMFORD 1939

BRENTWOOD

Wanstead   X

Y1

Leyton

Leyton-
stone

Gidea Park

ROMFORD X

Forest Gate

Whitechapel

Stratford

HORNCHURCH
STATION

CORBETS TEY

704

TUNBRIDGE WELLS

ROUTES 704 & 705
AFTER DIVERSION OF
705 THROUGH HAYES
1958

ALDGATE X Y1 Y2   Y2   Y2

Redcar. D was operated with Regals.

The arrival of the Southern Electric services at Sevenoaks via Orpington and via Swanley on 6 January 1935 changed the balance of rail and road service provision. Redcar sold out in February to Maidstone and District which maintained the Tunbridge Wells to London timings until Green Line took them over on 1 August. The services through Sevenoaks were rationalised on 8 January 1936, a half-hourly service operating between Tunbridge Wells and London throughout the week (on what were now C1 and C2). On 9 February 1938 route D ceased to work to Sevenoaks, being curtailed at Westerham except for garage journeys which continued to Dunton Green.

With war imminent, Green Line was suspended on 1 September 1939 and a double-deck bus route, 403D, ran half-hourly between Sevenoaks and Tunbridge Wells. As this was not the prime traffic flow it was not greatly patronised, suffering also from inability to pick up or set down passengers between Tonbridge and Tunbridge Wells. However, route C was restored between Tunbridge Wells and Chertsey, to run half-hourly on

Above right: Over 20 years since it first appeared at Sevenoaks, RF28 is seen at the Bus Station substituting for an RP. Leyland Nationals are much in evidence in December 1976. *Edward Shirras*

Right: Unmodernised RF214 works a 705 journey in 1973. Its London Country ownership is made manifest by the advertisement plastered on its nearside. *Edward Shirras*

3 March 1940. Later that year C was replaced by 5 to run from Victoria as a double-deck operation. It is interesting to note that from 1933 coaches from Sevenoaks (and Tunbridge Wells) had worked via Westminster Bridge, Horse Guards Avenue and then Eccleston Bridge – doubtless on the assumption that many civil servants lived in these favoured parts of Kent. Wartime route 5 continued this tradition until closure on 29 September 1942.

At the postwar restoration, Green Line provided four coaches hourly between Sevenoaks and London, two on 704 (to Windsor) and 705 (also to Windsor, via Westerham). The 10T10s were superseded on 1 October 1951 by the RFs put

into Green Line service, an indication that these routes were regarded as prestigious ones. Further evidence of this came with the appearance of the RC coaches on 705 on 28 November 1965, their dramatic new livery foretelling a new age for Green Line. They did not last long, however, being displaced by double-deck vehicles, RCLs, which were allocated to both routes on 2 December 1967. These coaches were very seldom occupied by full complements of passengers and the services were reduced to hourly workings on each route by the beginning of the London Country era, a very respectable provision even so. One-man operated coaches, initially RPs, duly appeared in 1972, though other vehicles, more or less suitable, were pressed into service as problems of availability became evident.

Routes 704 and 705 continued in being until they were almost the last of the 1946 scheme still maintained in their entirety, even if by somewhat make-shift means. However, further economies became necessary and in the fullness of time 705 disappeared except as a rather freakish Sunday working, the new timetable starting 20 May 1978. The hourly departures to Windsor were however maintained until 27 April 1979 when Tunbridge Wells and Windsor suffered a divorce after 33

Above: RCL2253 pauses at Langley on the A4 on its way from Windsor to Victoria, Westerham and Sevenoaks. Vehicles of this type worked 705 after the departure of the RC coaches in December 1967. *Edward Shirras*

Above right: The nadir of London Country's vehicular misfortunes was probably marked by the need to allocate this battered little Bristol to the formerly prestigious 704. There appears to be only one passenger who will probably not travel by Green Line again. The date: December 1976. *Edward Shirras*

Right: A view of the former Hillman garage in Romford in November 1936, before the arrival of new vehicles had swept away the Gilfords and the early T-types. The extent of Green Line commitment to the East London services is evident. Immediately before closure of the premises in 1977 only six coaches were housed there. *London Transport*

years of continuous association. The 704, re-numbered 706, now works only between Tunbridge Wells (West Station – not Limehill Road) and Victoria. A generous vehicle allocation at Dunton Green allows lengthy lay-over time at Eccleston Bridge, and the reliability of the service is likely to be greatly improved. Given the current needs of passengers to and from Sevenoaks these latest changes give the best promise of success.

Quite different is the position at Romford where

no trace remains of a once-busy service and almost frenzied activities of the early days. Romford is of course a contrast with Sevenoaks; few wish to travel to Romford to begin pleasurable walks, though the shops and market undoubtedly attract large numbers of people. It is a town almost wholly swallowed by a great mass of 1930s estate building added to in the 1950s so that the population has trebled in the period 1930 to 1960. Many of the people resident in Romford work in the City and were disadvantaged by having to travel in what became regarded, perhaps unjustly, as the most antiquated rail service of any London line. The steam operated trains gave way to frequent electric trains in 1949, but they did not cut into parallel Green Line traffic for many years; the collapse came much later, in the 1970s, and was complete when it came. A service that in 1965 needed 20 65-seater RCLs fell away to a half-hourly provision between Brentwood and London from 29 January 1977; the withdrawal was inevitable and was effected on 1 July in that year.

However, the beginning was rich with promise. In December 1928 Edward Hillman inaugurated a fast service between Stratford and Brentwood which was soon extended to Chelmsford and beyond. His blue and white Gilford coaches were subject to keen competition in the following year when Evans' Coaches began working Stratford to Brentwood and Mile End to Chelmsford and Sunset Pullman Saloons put on a Charing Cross to Brentwood service. In March 1930 Benjamin Davis started a Stratford to Brentwood operation, but in October 1930 Evans and Benjamin Davis became Eastward Coaches, a firm in which Edward Hillman had an interest. Thus, by mid-

1930 Edward Hillman and his associates were running a 10-minute service from Bow to Romford and Brentwood, while Sunset Saloons were running every 15 minutes over the same road but from Charing Cross. Green Line began operations on 23 July 1930 between Charing Cross Embankment and Brentwood at first every 20 minutes, by early 1931 every 6 to 12 minutes as far as Romford and Gidea Park, every 10 to 15 minutes to Brentwood.

Such frequency was not found anywhere else on Green Line and suggests that the coach services operated to Romford and Brentwood filled an identified, specific need. The independents on the road were acquired by the LPTB on

10 January 1934 and some 40 Gilford coaches, formerly Hillman, became Green Line. By 1936 Y1 was offering a coach every 3 minutes from Aldgate at peak hours to Romford, every seven minutes to Brentwood; (the off-peak frequencies were seven and 15 respectively). On Monday to Friday evenings, Saturday afternoons and evenings and Sundays Y1 coaches started at Horse Guards Avenue, a facility that was withdrawn on 6 October 1937. An additional, alternative service was provided between Romford and Aldgate by route X which began working via Eastern Avenue on 25 October 1933. Frequency eventually settled down to every 15 to 20 minutes. A special feature of all the routes through East London was the

Above: 721 was worked by single-deck, one-man-operated vehicles after the departure of the RCL class on 31 December 1971. This is LNC25 seen soon after delivery in 1973. There are uncomfortable seats for 49 passengers though they were seldom all occupied. *Edward Shirras*

special fare scale which allowed considerably cheaper travel than anywhere else in the LPTB area. The withdrawal of Green Line just before the outbreak of war caused considerable hardship and the Brentwood service was reinstituted on 1 November 1939 using double-deck vehicles (replacing the resplendent TFs that had appeared earlier in the year); route X followed on 18 December 1940. When the services vanished again on 29 September 1942 there were fewer passengers to be inconvenienced.

Operations between Aldgate and Brentwood began again on 6 March 1946, double-deck vehicles being confirmed in office; route X never reappeared. While the service provided on what was now 721 never equalled the prewar frequency, it was nonetheless on a short headway; basically a 10-minute through service was provided, supplementary coaches to and from Romford making a five-minute service at peak hours. Although the long-promised electric trains began running from Shenfield to Liverpool Street on 26 September 1949, Green Line held on to its share of the market until the early sixties. Daimler vehicles gave way to RTs; these in turn gave way

to RCL – long Routemaster Coaches – in 1965, but by this time the viability of the service was doubtful. Single-deck coaches with one-man operation were introduced in 1972; the service continued to wither, becoming half-hourly on 29 January 1977. Finally, and inevitably, it was withdrawn on 1 July 1977 and Romford garage, the centre of the former Hillman empire, was closed. Latterly the coaches trundling empty from Brentwood and through Romford were an uncomfortably sad sight.

Thus Romford has lost all its links with London by Green Line. In 1939 at the peak period some 24 coaches per hour were available between the Market Place in Romford and Aldgate (4 on X and 20 on Y). (At Ilford these were joined by another 12 coaches from Hornchurch and Corbets Tey on Y2). Of all these not a trace now remains. The only sight of a Green Line in Romford at the present time is of the hourly departures (every two hours on Sundays) of 712 and 713 for Harlow and Bishops Stortford. This semi-local route is the lineal descendant of the rather more prestigious peripheral 724 which ran from Romford to High Wycombe when it opened in 1966, a destination subsequently changed to Windsor. Very radical changes in travel patterns have taken place and these have brought about the collapse of the services on the London road. Clearly, many travellers have found more attractive alternatives.

14 Vehicles

The LGOC began their express operations with vehicles from their private hire fleet, including the following:

ADC (Associated Daimler Company) Type 419

LGOC purchased eight of these vehicles in 1926 and another 33 in 1927. They were designated 'All Weather Coaches' and numbered AW1 – 41; they had open coach bodies with folding hoods that had to be manoeuvred over the whole length of the car. AW1 – 8 were sold in 1929, so it is unlikely that they saw express duty; the others were rebuilt in 1930 by Short Brothers and given a semi-saloon coach body.

ADC Type 416

LGOC purchased 14 of these coaches in 1928 and allocated four to National. They were distinguished by their flat roofs, part of which folded back. The indicator was a small board fitted into brackets at the front of the roof structure. The ADC vehicles of both types were seen in the early days of express working, and appeared as Green Line reliefs (occasionally as service coaches) up to 1934. There were also two smaller Type 427 coaches.

R Type (AEC Reliance)

LGOC introduced 20 of these vehicles in 1929; they seated 32 passengers in a saloon which could be opened to the sky. Five more were obtained in 1930, to seat 28 passengers, and nine transferred from National were given coach bodies. That made up the class group R1 – 34, all the vehicles being used for private hire or express, later Green Line, work. A further nine were brought into the fleet on transfer from Batten's Coaches in late 1933; these became R35 – 43. All had ended their Green Line careers by 1935. They were sturdy looking vehicles with singularly dominating headlights.

The following vehicles were purpose-built for coach operation:

T-Type

This was an extremely long-serving classification in London's transport history. All the single-deck vehicles in this class were based on the AEC Regal chassis, type 662. T38, one of an order for 50 buses in 1929, was fitted with an experimental 28-seat saloon body especially designed for coach work. This was the prototype for the following production runs:

T51 – 149, 155, 157 – 206 (designated 7T7, total 150): introduced in 1930 they had six-cylinder petrol engines and 27-seat rear-entrance coach bodies built by the LGOC, Short Brothers and Hall Lewis. The first 40 appeared in red and black livery, the rest in green; 17 were allocated to East Surrey and nine to Autocar. In 1931 five were transferred to Amersham and District (these were T69, 71, 89, 96, 104), put into that company's livery for duty on the Chesham route until 1933. The gaps in the numbers are explained as follows: 150 – 154 were canvas-hooded private hire coaches which occasionally appeared on Green Line service; 156 was a bus, replacing T38.

T207 – 306, designated 1/7T7/1, introduced 1930/31, were the second series of coaches for Green Line. They differed from the first group in that the door was at the front (where it has always remained) and 'Green Line' appeared *below* the indicator at the front of the vehicle rather than above it. The emergency door was at the back. Coachwork was by Duple (50 coaches), Ransome (25) and Weymann (25). Oil engines were tried out in this series, T216, 274 and 305 being fitted with AEC Acro engines, later replaced by the AEC 8.8-litre Ricardo units. These coaches appeared somewhat

high off the road and slightly cumbersome; they were somewhat slow in acceleration by modern standards but the ride was not without quality. They, with the 7T7s, were the mainstay of the Green Line fleet until 1936 when they began to give way to more modern vehicles.

Above: A first series T in light green livery. It was of pleasingly austere appearance; the fussy LGOC curtains have gone, as have the destinations on the louvres. The roof boards were characteristic of all Green Line vehicles in the thirties. *London Transport*

Below: Q188, the experimental double-deck Green Line coach was introduced in 1936. It looked impressively modern but was not successful in service. *London Transport*

Acquired T-Types

A number of coaches acquired by Green Line and the LPTB were allocated numbers in the T series. These included T307 and 308 from Bucks Express, T309 – 24 from East Surrey, T346 – 51 from Blue Belle, T352 – 7 from Queen Line and T358 from Aston (Watford). To confuse matters somewhat, T325 – 45 were Autocar vehicles which never came to the LPTB, passing to Maidstone and District instead, and T307 – 18 were later (1935) renumbered T391 – 402. Then T359 – 68 came from Amersham and District and Lewis (Watford). Many of these ran as Green Line coaches. There was considerable variety and quality of coachwork.

Gilford Type Coaches, Coded GF

The Gilford coach, in its several versions, was basically a market-filler, a fairly cheaply devised vehicle that was produced in some numbers in 1928 and immediately after. It appealed to operators who were seeking equipment urgently in order to mount new services. They were beneath the dignity of the LGOC but were acquired by Green Line in considerable numbers from operators like Skylark (18 coaches), Regent (4), Bucks Express (5), Acme (14) and West London Coaches (3). In all, Green Line received 51 into its fleet before 1 July 1933. After that date, with the compulsory purchases made by the LPTB, Hillman surrendered some 57 Gilfords, Sunset Pullman 12, Upminster Services 24. In all 125 of these coaches were operated by Green Line; 112 astonishingly were still listed in 1935. With the advent of new vehicles of LPTB design in the following year, however, they were quickly removed. The GF numbering scheme is incredibly confusing as it was done twice. Quite early in their careers these coaches took on a shabby gentility that implied readiness for the breaker's yard somewhat prematurely.

Leyland Coaches

Green Line acquired a number of Leyland vehicles and put them into an L class in 1932, these being Lion, Tiger and Titan models some of which went back to 1927. The Lions were all-weather coaches and did not survive long enough to be reclassified in 1935 when the Titans became TD and the Tigers TR. Former Premier Line vehicles included 19 Titans (TD132, 174 – 91) – the single-deck version was a rarity – and 18 Tigers (TR2 – 5 and 18 – 31). TR11 – 17 were ex-Maidstone and District, TR32 – 35 were luxurious coaches from Prince Omnibus Co. Finally, TR36 – 40 were originally Redcar coaches, later Maidstone and District vehicles, that were transferred to the LPTB in 1935. Most of these coaches appeared on Green Line service; the majority worked from Northfleet and Staines on A1 and A2, and from Addlestone and Tunbridge Wells for the C routes. They appeared somewhat primitive vehicles, ruggedly austere. They lasted until 1938 when they were replaced by the 10T10s – a contrast indeed.

Miscellaneous Acquisitions

During the period of Green Line take-over in 1932, and later after the implementation of the London Passenger Transport Act, many odd makes of coach were added to stock. These included one Albion, one Bedford and one GMC, the latter an all-weather coach; there were two Commer

Below: The 9T9 coach that appeared in 1936. Its built-up wing structure gave it a modern look that was largely nullified by the rather flimsy bumper. They were smart vehicles but never really powerful enough for Green Line operation. *London Transport*

vehicles and two Daimlers, two Morris vehicles and two Saurers. Two Maudslays (ML3 type) came from Bucks Express and two others from the GWR. There were five Dennis vehicles and six Tilling-Stevens, together with three examples of the Thornycroft. Most of these were drafted into the private hire fleet – which must have been remarkable for its variety – and thus some may have found themselves as Green Line reliefs. However, these venerable vehicles were quickly removed from stock when standard coaches became available.

Q Type

Q189 – 238, total 50. This was an AEC design, advanced for its time, with the normal oil engine mounted, slightly inclined, on the off-side of the chassis behind the driver's cab. The Green Line version, 6Q6, appeared in late 1936; it seated 32 in a Park Royal body. They were distinguishable from bus versions not only because of the livery but by the radiator grill – actually an air intake – on the front of the coach. These were fast-moving, almost nippy vehicles, though slightly claustrophobic perhaps because the win-

Left: Posed before taking up duty, the pleasing lines of the 10T10 are displayed in this view of T505. This coach, displaced by the RFs in 1951, became a red Central bus for a short period before withdrawal. *London Transport*

Below left: The TF coach arrived on the scene in 1939. The darker livery then current is apparent. The design inheritance from the 10T10 is evident at the rear, though the front end is totally new to take advantage of fitting the engine flat underneath the floor — a revolutionary concept. *London Transport*

Right: The entrance to RF26 — it will be noted that the floor level is quite high. The plate to the left of the running numbers allowed for the fitting of semaphore signal equipment, though few vehicles were so provided. *London Transport*

Below right: An impressive full-front view of RT3236 at Aldgate shortly after vehicles of this class took over 721 in June 1950. The bodies were built by Weymann. *London Transport*

dows seemed very small. Initially they worked Hertford to Guildford (the M group) and Q and R; all were ambulances during the war and on resumption of Green Line duly reappeared for the Hertford to Guildford service. They were undoubtedly a successful design of vehicle.

9T9 Type

T403 – 452, introduced in 1936, were 30-seat coaches with Weymann bodies and distinguished by the building of the near-side wing structure into the engine cover. The engine, the 7.7 litre, was not really up to coach performance though these vehicles worked I and J (Crawley/Reigate to Watford and Abbots Langley) and others until drafted to Country bus work. Some took up Green Line duty postwar but only for a short time.

10T10 Type

T453 – 718 (total 266), introduced 1938. These coaches set a new standard for Green Line and were its most distinguished vehicles prewar. A larger engine, 8.8 litre, was used compared with its predecessor and the coachwork was Chiswick-design and build; the first coaches delivered seated 30, later ones (1/10T10/1) were equipped with 34 seats. They combined solidity with style and rapidly identified Green Line operation. Some became ambulances and others served the American Army during the war. On resumption of Green Line in 1946 they were the standard vehicles. There was a quality of ride quite unique; however, some of the seating was seemingly never secured after the wartime removal and there was a

tendency for loose equipment to clatter from time to time. They were immensely popular with crews and travelling public alike.

TF Type

TF14 – 88, introduced 1939, Leyland chassis, Chiswick-built coaches seating 34. This was a most advanced vehicle for its time, the first in public service with the engine, an 8.6-litre unit, on its side under the floor. They were handsome coaches, allocated at first to Romford and Grays. All were ambulances during the war and returned to take up Green Line duty at St Albans, Dorking and Luton (for 712, 713, and 714). They did not live a full life – technically advanced with fluid flywheel, pre-selective gearbox and air operated

Left: The Routemaster coach, RMC class, was introduced on the 715 in 1962. These powerful vehicles proved their worth in rapid acceleration and reliability. Their interiors were well-adapted to Green Line requirements, though they never presented the ambience of the coach. *London Transport*

Below left: Side-by-side: RCL2246 on 723 is about to leave followed by RMC1496 now relegated to bus work on route 370. Green Line coaches no longer appear at the Tilbury Riverside terminus. *Edward Shirras*

Below: The RC class worked the 727 for a time; they lost four seats behind the driver and luggage racks were installed. Here RC9 pulls away from Watford Junction in May 1969. *Edward Shirras*

gear changing and braking systems, spare parts became a source of anxiety for so small a build of vehicle. In postwar years it was possible to detect a 1930s design only by the eliptical wheel guards.

D Type (Daimler)

D133 – 7, 141, 143 – 9, 151 – 4, 156 – 9, 161, 164 – 70, 172 – 9 (37 vehicles). These were basically wartime double-deck buses; Daimler CWA6 chassis with STL-type engines were fitted with a Duple body immediately after the war when regulations were relaxed a little to allow a small degree of refinement. They were allocated to Romford in 1946 for 721 and 722 and did yeoman work out of Aldgate. A further 5 (D67, 68, 69, 71 and 73) arrived at Romford in December 1948, ex-Central bus fleet. A curiosity is that these squarely-built, crude-looking vehicles did not encourage their passengers to find other means of travel, bearing in mind that their prewar predecessors on these East London routes were the TFs.

RT Type (AEC Regent)

RT3224 – 3259 (36 vehicles, coded 3RT8/1, introduced 1950) replaced the D type vehicles at Romford – doubtless to the relief of crews and passengers. These double-deck vehicles with Weymann bodies looked especially distinguished in Green Line livery. An additional batch of 21

vehicles, RT4489 – 4509, arrived at Grays in October 1953 to take over the 723 routes while 28 others were received in 1951/2 and 1960.

RF Type
AEC Regal Mark IV chassis with 9.6-litre underfloor engine and Metro-Cammel-Weymann bodywork, coded 1/2RF2/1. Introduced in 1951, this coach immediately proved its worth and became

standard equipment for Green Line displacing all other single-deck types. The first 30ft-long coaches, they seated 39 passengers. A novelty was the mechanically-operated door, an innovation welcomed by conductors. RF26 – 288 (263 coaches) were allocated to Green Line, but service requirements in 1956 brought about the transfer of six from the Central fleet, together with 19 former Country buses to Green Line, making 288 in all. The transferred vehicles were appropriately equipped, furnished and painted. Additionally, 10RFs originally allocated to private hire, 27ft long, seating 35 and with glass-panelled roofs, were moved to Green Line work. The renumbering scheme for these coaches caused corresponding changes in Central and Country bus lists. 175 were modernised, the programme being completed in 1967; the styling and livery were brought up to date. They have proved almost incredibly sturdy and reliable vehicles (the counterparts of the RTs, many of whose components they share) and some were still at work for Green Line in 1978.

Left: RTs have a long record of work as Green Line reliefs. Brands Hatch is now served by special journeys on occasional route 739, but while Wrotham was the destination of the 719, additional journeys were provided by RTs sent up from Swanley. RT3333 awaits departure from Buckingham Palace Road. *Edward Shirras*

Below: A stormy day and the evening sun highlight two Alexander-bodied AEC Swifts on the 725 at Windsor. SMA17 and SMA14 (to the rear) spent most of their time on this service. *Edward Shirras*

RMC Type – the Routemaster Coach

Experimental use of prototype CRL4 convinced Green Line that the future lay in double-deck operation and 68 of these splendid vehicles were ordered for delivery in 1962. RMC1453 – 1520, plus CRL4 now renumbered RMC4, took over 715 and other routes where passenger numbers justified the change from single-deck coaches. Seats were provided for 57 passengers, 25 on the lower deck, 32 upstairs and furnishings were to a high standard. In service, the RMCs proved as formidably aggressive as their Central bus counter-parts, though technical modifications to the suspension ensured a rather more comfortable ride. There were advantages of improved visibility for Green Line travellers upstairs, but in the long term it is doubtful if a double-deck vehicle was entirely appropriate for coach work. In any case, shortly after they were delivered passenger journeys began to fall. Chassis were AEC; bodies, designed at Chiswick, were built by Park Royal.

RCL Type

Longer versions of the Routemaster were built to 30ft, these vehicles being readily identifiable by the additional small windows inserted midway along the body. An 11.3-litre AEC engine was fitted; coachwork was again Park Royal. Classi-fied 8RM10, 43 of these coaches were ordered for the Romford and Grays routes and took up duties in 1965 though initially the Grays allocation could not be worked there and were transferred. Seats were provided for 65 passengers in much the same style as the RMC. Because of their size they became something of an embarrassment; some were employed in other services such as the 704. They were characteristically splendid machines, emphasising the point that London was best served by buses specifically built to withstand its traffic conditions. With the end of Routemaster production shortly after these vehicles were built the long association of London Transport with AEC ended.

RC Type

AEC Reliances, with a characteristic Willowbrook body, these coaches were delivered in 1965 and took up duties on 705. Nearly 36ft long they were distinguished by long side windows and a new colour scheme for Green Line, light grey with a broad green band. They seated 49 passen-gers. They were not very reliable and not popular with crews; they were withdrawn after two years but reinstated on other services in standard livery; they worked 727 for a while. RC1 – 14 lost one of their number, RC11, which was badly damaged in a fire arising from engine malfunction. This type was something of a failure, clearly lacking the stamina needed for Green Line work.

Below: SMA8, newly delivered, does brisk business in North Cheam. *Edward Shirras*

It will be noted that most types of coach on Green Line work during the London Transport era were matched with successful double-deck designs; hence the 10T10 derived in part from the STL, the RF from the RT. The Routemaster (RM) never had a single deck version, though one (RM1368) was constructed after fire had destroyed the upper deck. It looked quite hideous and it is pleasing to think it did not appear in Green Line colours. With the formation of London Country, 1 January 1970, the links with London-type vehicles were severed so far as new deliveries were concerned. The purchasing policy was dominated by expediency as it was a matter of urgency that some replacements for existing stock should be made as soon as possible.

RP Type

AEC Reliances with Park Royal coach bodies seating 45 were delivered in 1971/2 in order to replace all double-deck working on Green Line (except for 709). RP1 – 90 are not very attractive vehicles being more akin to a bus than a coach, though all are equipped with luggage racks and an air conditioning system. They tend to look somewhat heavy from side-view and the front is dominated by the steering column assembly. RP7, 46 and 87 have had the doubtful privilege of appearing with all-over advertisements; thus RP7 extolled the virtues of Champion Sparking Plugs in March 1973.

SMA Type

The SMA class was based on the AEC Swift chassis with Alexander coachwork. These coaches, seating 45, were originally ordered by South Wales Transport but diverted to London Country where

they were set to work on the 725. Not unpleasing in appearance, they tended to be underpowered – the engine is rated at 8.2 litre – and are less than ideal for Green Line schedules. SMA1 – 21 were delivered in 1972.

LNB/LNC Class
The introduction of Leyland National buses on Green Line in 1972/3 marked the nadir of vehicle provision for the service. The LNC differed from the bus (LNB) version only in external livery; the interior remained entirely standard. These vehicles, at 37ft 2in, were the longest ever operated by Green Line, and the noisiest. They did a great deal of damage to the Green Line image in the short period they worked on coach routes. Most of the group LNB/C24 – 70 were on coach duties until replaced by the shorter versions, the SNB/SNC classes. They seated 49 passengers.

SNB Class
These were buses delivered 1974/5, SNB71 – 115 being allocated to Green Line as a temporary measure until the SNCs became available. They seated 41 in minimum comfort.

SNC Class
Some attempt, not unsuccessful, was made to ameliorate the bare interiors of the standard Leyland and to improve seating (for 39 passengers). Luggage racks and high-backed seats were fitted, making some amends for previous deliveries. SNC116 – 202 (87 coaches) were in general Green Line service, though by 1979 the number was much reduced.

RB and RS Classes
These are coaches based on the AEC Reliance 760 chassis; RB are Duple Dominant – the B stands for Blackpool – RS are Plaxton Supreme coaches built at Scarborough. The new livery adopted is very pleasing, the only weakness of design appearing to be the limited space for destination blinds. They are undoubtedly very smart vehicles, hopefully eye-catching enough to restore the Green Line image. They began on the Airports service 727 and on the express Windsor workings on 700; they have now (summer 1979) been allocated to all daily routes except the 'local' routes from Bishops Stortford to Walthamstow and Romford and the Aldgate/Grays service. They seat 49 passengers in air-conditioned comfort (while the vehicle is in motion, that is); the orange decor is pleasing and the large windows offer excellent viewing when London Country have not stuck notices on them. Drivers find them somewhat hot 'up-front' but good vehicles to handle. Five of the 120 vehicles in these classes have been given special transfer treatment for the non-stop 747 Jetlink service between Gatwick and London Airports.

Experimental Vehicles
This list should legitimately begin with T38, the LGOC's first attempt to devise an appropriate vehicle for express coach work. It had a 28-seat

rear-entrance body built at Chiswick and entered service between Golders Green and Watford in January 1930. It was the prototype for the successful 7T7 series.

LT1137 was a six-wheel double-deck coach based on the AEC Renown chassis. Chiswick-built, it had a sunshine roof, seats for 50 passengers, a front entrance and a rear staircase. In appearance it was somewhat threatening. Introduced in September 1931 on route E (Bushey to Crawley) it was withdrawn from Green Line the following year, being far too ponderous for express working.

Q188 was another six-wheel, double-deck experiment based on the Q principle. This was a more handsome vehicle than LT1137 with the passenger door centrally placed in a body built by Park Royal. However, it worked on Green Line routes for only a short time.

TF1 might be regarded as an experiment, being an amalgam of Leyland and LPTB expertise. As built the driver's cab was virtually a glasshouse. Its success was followed by production runs of Private Hire coaches (TF2 – 13) and the Green Line coaches already listed.

RTC1 was a reconstruction of RT97 which had sustained bomb damage and the design was based on 'pay-as-you-enter' principles. A conductor sat at the rear entrance facing a cash register. Luxury seating was provided for 46 passengers and additional features were a power-operated sliding door, an elaborate heating system and fluorescent lighting. The coach appeared in 1949 on several routes but conclusions drawn from its use at the time did not favour double-deck working except on 721 and 722.

CRL4 was the prototype Routemaster coach; Leyland mechanical units were fitted with an Eastern Coachworks body. Introduced in October 1957, the successful operation of this vehicle led to the building of the RMC class.

Perhaps mention should be made of the rather bizarre experiments conducted prior to the introduction of the RF coaches. A Q-type vehicle, mocked up to RF dimensions, worked every Green Line route to satisfy the police and licensing authorities that so long a vehicle could be worked satisfactorily. It did not carry passengers.

London Country now (summer 1979) operate 17 AEC Reliance coaches carrying the fleet name 'Green Line', though they are confined to touring or private hire work and are allocated to National Express for summer services. They are coded D (for Duple) or P (for Plaxton) who built the luxury coach bodies. They are not equipped for scheduled Green Line duties.

Left: Some SNC workings were inserted into the 725 schedule as an interim between the SMA class and the arrival of the new RB/RS coaches. SNC169 arrives at Windsor Coach Station. *Edward Shirras*

Below: In eye-catching new livery, Hatfield-based RS42 picks up passengers at Brent Cross en route to Hitchin on the 732. At last Green Line again has a prestigious vehicle allocated to its services. *Edward Shirras*

15 Garages

The first LGOC express coaches began work from Brixton Private Hire garage (coded BT), formerly Cambrian Landray which opened in 1927, and from premises in Leavesden Road, Watford (WT) dating from 1920. Having fallen into disuse, Watford was reopened specifically for coach operation in 1929. Other LGOC establishments involved in express working were Slough, Alpha Street (SL), opened in 1926, concerned with the Windsor service started in 1930, and Maidenhead which was used for coaches only between August and October 1930 when it closed. Of these garages, Brixton ceased to be used for express coaches shortly after the formation of Green Line Coaches Ltd when the LGOC operations were transferred to out-London bases; it remained operational for private hire, however, until 1938. Alpha Road, Slough was closed in 1933 after the refusal of licences for routes M and Z. Watford, on the other hand, flourished and, raised to the status of a Coach Station, became a major centre of Green Line activity. On the withdrawal of Green Line on 31 August 1939, however, it lost its role immediately and entirely and never again serviced a coach; closure came in 1952.

With the setting up of services by the various companies acting as agents of the LGOC a number of garages in Autocar and East Surrey territory were involved in coach operation. The Tunbridge Wells service operated from the main Autocar depot (opened in 1914). With the advent of the LPTB these premises passed to Maidstone and District, who still use them. Green Line kept a foothold in Tunbridge Wells, really some way beyond the LPTB boundary, by acquiring a small garage, later coded TW, which Autocar had formerly used for private hire work. Used as a store during the war, TW reopened in 1946 with an allocation of nine coaches. It was closed and disposed of in 1967 after the 704 base was moved

to Dunton Green. One vehicle on this service however is still housed overnight in Tunbridge Wells by M. and D.

It should perhaps be noted at this point that the LGOC system of coding garages, dating from 1912, also applied to Green Line and Country Bus duty schedules from the early days. The code plates themselves did not appear on the vehicles until late 1934 when coaches were given running numbers for the first time. However, for the sake of clarity, codes are indicated for all garages mentioned.

East Surrey's first base, Reigate (RG), was established before World War I in 1912, extended several times and provided coaches for the service to London on 6 June 1930. Always the centre of operations, Reigate is the administrative headquarters of London Country today. The LGOC established a number of well-placed garages across East Surrey territory and these were used by the Company. This group comprised Dunton Green (DG), opened in 1922, and Swanley (SJ), Godstone (GD), Chelsham (CM) and Leatherhead (LH), all of which became operational in 1925. East Grinstead (EG – opened 1925) and Crawley (CY – 1929 were built from the Company's own resources. Dorking (DS) was built in 1931. All these garages were involved in coach operating from the beginning, though Leatherhead did not service coaches after the war and Chelsham ceased to be concerned with daily Green Line in 1977. All have been extended and rebuilt over the years, the principal contribution of the LPTB being the handsome administrative blocks exemplified by the premises at Swanley. Early garages were places for vehicles, lacking the amenities for human beings that bus crews now, very properly, expect.

In 1931 East Surrey took over the LGOC garage at Crayford (CR) which was opened in 1917 to provide buses for munitions workers. The Dart-

ford (later, Gravesend) services were worked from this depot until 1934; the premises were closed and sold shortly afterwards. One wall of the building is still visible in what is now a petrol station.

North of the Thames National had their own bases at Bishops Stortford (opened 1919) and Hitchin. They acquired Ware (built 1921) from Harvey and Burrows in 1924 and leased Hatfield which the LGOC built in 1922. All these garages were involved in the initiation of Green Line services in 1930. Later, coaches on the London/Bishops Stortford route ran from the former Acme garage acquired in 1932 and coded BS until closure in 1934 with the opening of Epping. At Hitchin the position was reversed, the LPTB gaining complete control. Ware closed in 1935 on the opening of Hertford. Hatfield (HF) was rebuilt

Left: T255 receives attention at Addlestone (WY) garage before taking up duty on C2 between Woking and Tunbridge Wells. The Kentish hills made this route a demanding proposition for this type of vehicle. *London Transport*

Below: A view of the former Premier Line garage in Bath road, Slough, in July 1936. The Premier origin of three of the Leyland coaches is clearly indicated by the large roof-box destination indicators. The round sterns and dangling starting handles are very much part of the period. *London Transport*

on a site across the road in 1959 and is still operational; Hitchin (HN) closed in 1959 with the development of full facilities at Stevenage (SV).

The Harpenden service opened on 20 September 1930 was based on the Comfy Cars depot in London Road, Harpenden, a firm with whom Green Line had entered into agreement. The garage was quoted as a Green Line enquiry office in early leaflets and was later acquired by the LPTB on 6 February 1934. It continued to house Green Line vehicles until later that year when they were transferred to Luton (LS).

Certain garages were opened expressly for Green Line work in 1930. Initially of very economical construction, usually of corrugated iron, they were extended in the thirties and given full facilities by the LPTB. This group includes Addlestone (WY), Guildford (GF) and Staines (ST), all of which quickly added bus operations to their responsibilities. Incidentally, services were started before the garages were available and coaches had to be housed in the Weymann works at Addlestone, in a yard adjacent to the London Road Railway Station in Guildford and in a works yard at Staines in the first few months. Romford, North Street, coded RF, was a small depot which was used to develop the Brentwood service; it was retained when the Hillman premises became

Above: An interior view of Northfleet garage (NF) shortly after opening in 1937. T240 receiving attention is, curiously, a C2 coach that would normally be dealt with at Tunbridge Wells or Addlestone. The photograph emphasises the space available in garages designed by the LPTB. *London Transport*

Above right: RF203 awaits departure on 725 in September 1955, by which time this peripheral route via Croydon to Windsor was well-established. The characteristic LPTB architecture of the mid-1930s remains pleasing; the extreme neatness of the entire garage complex reflects a high standard of management and care. *London Transport*

available, later being used for the coaches on route X. The present Central Bus garage, NS, dates from 1952. A curiosity of the time was the use of the AEC works at Southall as an operational depot for the Uxbridge service. This lasted from 7 February 1931 to 2 January 1934 when vehicles were transferred to Amersham and High Wycombe. The Sunbury route was run from a small garage in Hanworth Road, Sunbury, actually part of the premises of a mineral water firm; when the coaches were put through to Staines in January 1934 the depot became redundant.

In the series of acquisitions in 1932, Green Line secured two garages which serviced the Associated Coaches operation to Ongar. One was in Bridge Street, Ongar, the other in New Road, South Chingford, a former Lion Motor Services base. Chingford was operational for only a short time, the Ongar base being retained – despite its primitive nature – until the opening of Epping in

1934. The Chiltern Bus Service garage in Tring was acquired on 10 May 1933; this modest establishment was rebuilt by the LPTB and used for Green Line work continuously, except of course for the war, until its closure in 1977 during the London Country retreat. It was coded TG.

One garage was planned and opened during the period of the London General Country Services. This was Windsor (WR) which dates

from 1933. Extensions added in 1936 allowed the closing of Slough (SU). At various times the garage in St Leonards Road has been called a 'Coach Station.'

With the implementation of the London Transport Act, the Maidstone and District garage at Dartford passed immediately to the LPTB on 1 July 1933. Green Line coaches were, however, based there only in 1934 and 1935; in 1953 Dartford (DT) regained coach work when allocated four RFs for the increased service on 725. LPTB operations in Gravesend had initially to be carried out from the former tram sheds in Dover Road, Northfleet. The Amersham and District garages at Amersham and High Wycombe came into LPTB ownership on 1 October 1933. Coding these garages caused some problems as the obvious AM was already allocated to Plumstead, and HW to Hanwell. They became MA and HE respectively. Initially, High Wycombe, opened in

1928, had facilities for selling and servicing cars. MA was closed in 1935 on the opening of more extensive premises put up by the Board which have provided Green Line coaches ever since, albeit with a gap between 1972 and 1977. High Wycombe was closed in 1977.

On the Bath Road, the Premier garage which had begun coach operations in 1930 passed to the LPTB on 20 December 1933. It was complete with pumps and a public service forecourt. Coded SU it remained operational until coaches were transferred to Windsor in 1936. Another major Green Line base was secured by the acquisition of the Hillman Saloon Coaches premises in London Road, Romford in 1934. This extensive garage, known as RE, housed the large fleet of coaches provided for routes Y1 and Y2, and for post-war services 721 and 722. Closure came in 1977, at which point a mere six Leyland National vehicles were allocated. In 1934 also, London Transport

gained possession of the Strawhatter service from Luton together with the garage in Park Street West which became LS. With the shrinking of London Country's interest in this area in 1976 the establishment was closed after continuous association with Green Line working.

A major feature of LPTB planning was to secure a series of well-placed bases for bus and coach operation, especially north of the Thames. In this area depots were mainly small, often inconveniently sited. A major building programme was implemented and new premises were opened at Epping (EP) in 1934, Grays (GY), Hemel Hempstead (HH) and Hertford (HG) – all in 1935, and at St Albans (SA) in 1936. The opening of these bases allowed the closure of several smaller, inherited garages such as Ware and Ongar. Additionally, as has already been noted, new buildings were provided for Amersham in 1935; south of the Thames a new garage was established in London Road, Northfleet (NF) which became operational in 1936. Many of the other garages were given improved facilities and amenities in characteristic LPTB architecture.

Above: Two 704 reliefs arrive back at Windsor one summer Sunday in 1969. They are RT3118 and RML2436. Both look impressively well-kept. *Edward Shirras*

Above right: RMC1516 stands at Hatfield garage (HF) shortly after the London Country take-over and the removal of the London Transport sign. The old Hatfield garage stood on the opposite side of the road. *Edward Shirras*

Right: High Wycombe garage (HE) was formerly owned by Amersham and District. In the period that 724 worked there, RF183 (ex-coach now in bus livery) waits for time. The garage closed in 1977. *Edward Shirras*

After the war there were few developments until the opening of a new garage at Garston (GR) in June 1952; the closure of Watford, Leavesden Road quickly followed, though by that time no coaches were being operated. GR gained an allocation of RFs for Green Line work with the introduction of route 719 in 1956. This and other innovations were associated with the New Towns. A small, temporary shed was provided with four RFs at Stevenage (SV) in 1955 to facilitate improving the 716 service; new premises in

Danestreet opened in 1959 and Hitchin was closed. Further east, Harlow (HA) opened in 1963 and Epping closed in consequence as it was no longer the centre of the route system.

It has to be noted that the garages in London Transport days were almost clinically clean and neat. London Country have had the disadvantage of carrying out quite heavy engineering on their premises, with consequent deleterious effects on the environment. It is to be hoped that the opening of Tinsley Green will allow the concentration of dismantled (sometimes derelict) vehicles there and that the appearance of their premises will improve.

Apart from garages exclusively concerned with Green Line, coaches allocated to Country Bus garages shared the facilities with the buses. Crews were always separately identified and interchanges for bus working were rare in London Transport days, though an overtime journey on a bus route was sometimes added to the working day. Appearing on a Green Line roster was to be among an elite of busmen, though many thought of coach work as rather boring, limited in most cases to working one route and lacking the variety of country bus working. Through most of the 1950s and 1960s RT vehicles in full Green Line livery were used to duplicate morning and evening peak hour journeys to London. Green Line coaches occasionally turned up as Country buses, and vice versa if a coach was not available for duty. This caused some dismay to orthodox enthusiasts and

Above: Two SMA coaches on 725 stand in tandem at Windsor while intending passengers patiently wait for the doors to open. *Edward Shirras*

Above right: LNC31, unusually working a 724 journey to Romford in July 1973, is about to leave Staines garage. The architecture and the coach stop sign are plainly LPTB, though London Country are now in charge. *Edward Shirras*

Right: A sign of the times: an RB coach moves away from its stand at Windsor. The NBC sign on the roof of the building is less dramatically striking than the London Transport roundel that preceded it. *Edward Shirras*

minor inconvenience to travellers because of the lack of luggage racks. In London Country days, the desperate vehicle situation of the early and middle seventies made the allocating of coaches highly unpredictable. However, since the arrival of the RB and RS coaches a more uniform allocation of vehicles to the coach routes has been possible.

A missed journey before 1939 was almost unheard of and this happy situation continued in the postwar period for some years. The development of London Airport and the consequent acute shortage of labour north and west of London particularly has caused chronic staffing problems in the garages, especially Windsor and Staines. Missed journeys became commonplace in the sixties through lack of drivers to take the coaches out, and the unreliability of the service thus caused

became, without doubt, one of the reasons for the decline in passenger numbers.

Reference should be made at this point to the Green Line establishment at Western House, 237 – 239 Oxford Street which served both as an enquiry office and as the control centre of Green Line operations throughout the London Transport era. Here senior inspectors, men with expert knowledge of routes, vehicle running schedules and crew duties, maintained an overview of the whole system. Corrective action consequent on break-

down, accident or abnormal traffic delay was initiated by the controller; local action was discouraged except in emergencies. This facility ceased to be available to London Country who have a small hutch-like structure on Eccleston Bridge, though this is primarily for enquiry work and bookings for National coaches. Day-to-day supervision is maintained by road inspectors posted at key points throughout the London Country area and in London where they may be seen at Victoria, Oxford Circus and Hammersmith.

16 Green Line —
An Assessment

The history of Green Line covers a long period of change in the bus and coach industry and in the climate in which it has worked. Green Line began as an emulation of a final phase of private enterprise and was quickly brought within a framework of control; this control was achieved by two key Acts of Parliament – the Road Traffic Act of 1930 and the London Passenger Transport Act of 1933. Even if this legislative framework had not been created, commercial constraints would probably have proved as effective – during the 1930s the spheres of influence of most of the companies operating today were clearly defined.

It is interesting to note the caution with which

the LGOC entered the field of suburban semi-fast coach operation. What were the London General's competitors trying to prove? They were seeking to capture existing traffic from established operators – the LGOC buses and the main and Underground railways – and to create a new travelling public. In both aims they were undoubtedly successful, though the feverish competition engendered increased the number of coaches on the roads and the number of operators dramatically. Hence, profit margins were reduced and services withdrawn; there were few bankruptcies, the usual practice being to sell out to a rival at a financially critical (and advantageous) point. The entry of the LGOC

Below left: This mid 1930s view was characteristic of Green Line. A first series T-type coach on route C1 loads at Eccleston Bridge. Some of the passengers appear to have been waiting for a considerable time.
London Transport

Above: London Transport operation of Green Line in the late 1960s is exemplified by RF80 in gleaming order waiting to take a 719 working from Eccleston Bridge.
Edward Shirras

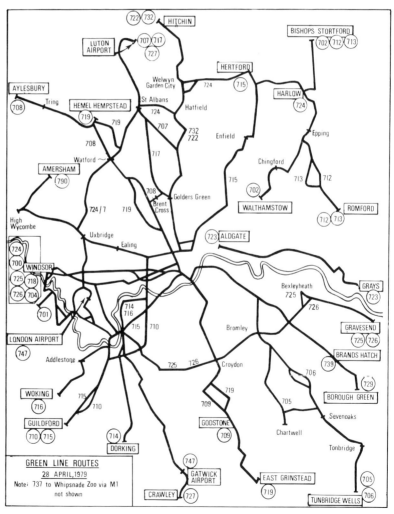

GREEN LINE ROUTES
28 APRIL,1979
Note: 737 to Whipsnade Zoo via M1 not shown

travellers that had played such a part in building up passenger clientele.

However, for many journeys in the 1930s Green Line was an attractive form of transport. Even in the area covered by the services of the Southern Railway much of the operation was by steam and services were relatively infrequent; electrification, which brought fast, frequent and regular-interval services, reached Dartford in 1926, Guildford in 1925, Gravesend in 1930, and Reigate in 1932. However, Sevenoaks was not reached by 'Southern Electric' until 1935, and Horsham in 1938. With the coming of revitalised rail services Green Line lost some of its advantages, suffering especially from relatively long journey times. Some thinning of services in Leatherhead (1937) and in Sevenoaks (1938) were presumably logical outcomes of improved rail facilities, skilfully marketed. Even so, Green Line presented a good image in LPTB days and held on to a sector of the travelling public who were remarkably loyal. There was great staff loyalty to the system as well, and one perhaps explains the other. Green Line travellers in the late 1930s were probably what National Trust members are supposed to be – middle-aged, middle-class and women. The quality of service provided by Green Line has always been based on professional, unfussy care of the passenger, and on the ambiance provided by the coach. These factors are still important though crews, passengers and decors have changed.

The demographic changes in the LPTB area have seemingly mattered less to Green Line than might have been expected. While the central zones have lost population, the 'Country area' has increased from 998,000 in 1933 to 2,389,000 in 1969. The importance of the suburban coach was accepted during the early part of the war, but one of the puzzles of postwar operation was the relatively limited role taken by Green Line at a time when all other forms of public transport were hard-pressed to carry their passengers. An unattractive fare scale was only one consideration in the quality aspects of Green Line that were still evident. One explanation may be that in the period when Green Line did not operate at all (1942 to 1946) passen-

into the coach business marked a new stage in the process: the immense resources of the combine were in contrast with the flimsy nature of many of the smaller operators. Thus the LGOC could pursue a policy relentlessly while its competitors succumbed; in this way most of the London independents' buses had disappeared in the late twenties. Doubtless LGOC saw the coach business as the scene of a similar battle. Once drawn in, the company attacked with vigour. It was fortunate to have two very determined men in charge of its affairs – Lord Ashfield and Frank Pick – and to have the organising and imaginative qualities of A. H. Hawkins to manage Green Line on the road.

The restoration of order was completed by the implementation of the London Transport Act (1933) and monopoly reasserted. Green Line became institutionalised but the coaches lost their prime function as a competitive facility in the financial sense. Doubtless those who rode on the coaches from Hertford and Guildford to Oxford Circus were attracted by the novelty of new technology – and were also originally attracted by fares that were less than comparable charges on railways or parallel bus services. The rationalisation of fares throughout the LPTB area meant that Green Line competed with other forms of transport on a convenience and quality basis. After the removal of coaches from Central London Green Line lost some of the convenience for gers became accustomed to rail travel, especially in the south, and developed travel habits they saw no reason to change after the war. As has been noted, a new fare scale in 1950 brought passenger figures up to respectable levels, and a new generation of Green Line traveller became identified.

It has always been something of a myth that Green Line passengers wished to travel to London or from London. Certainly in the 1950s the characteristic traveller occupied his seat in the outer-suburbs: he travelled towards London as far as Ealing, Golders Green, Bromley and Eltham. It became evident that much coach mileage in Central London was patently unremunerative. Except at peak hours (and sometimes not even then) the passenger stands at Victoria rarely saw queues; the stops at Baker Street and Oxford Circus were comparatively deserted. By this time, too, traffic congestion and vastly increased use of the car were telling against the bus industry generally, and especially against Green Line where so much of each cross-London journey was spent in battles for road space. The 292,000 cars registered in the Metropolitan Police Area in 1933 had become 2,285,000 by 1969. Unreliability through loss of time on journeys was readily accepted by the zealous Green Line traveller as a hazard of his journey. However, when other factors in the general malaise in public transport influenced Green Line travel in the late 1950s and 1960s, even the zealous found loyalty hard to maintain. Thus journeys were lost through shortage of crews, and services became suspect. There is little doubt that the greatest damage has been done to public service operations by the bus or coach that does not run. Frustrated travellers seek alternative ways of making their journeys, and improved rail facili-

ties north of London have matched those that had long been available on Southern Region (thus Enfield was reached by electric train in 1960, Amersham in 1961 and Harlow and Bishops Stortford in 1962; regular-interval services have been established by diesel trains on other lines).

The descending spiral, where falling passenger numbers induce lower frequencies of service which in turn encourage travellers to buy their own cars or go by train, has been a feature of Green Line operation since the early sixties. The collapse was all but completed by London Country's vehicle problems in the early 1970s. A complicating factor in any assessment of public transport operation currently is the provision of grant aid by Central Government (for new vehicles) or Local Government (for operating subsidies). It becomes difficult to discern the viability of a service and to assess its value as a facility. It is sometimes an over simplification to suggest that if passengers in sufficient numbers do not come forward to pay their fares then the service is not wanted, but this criterion must remain significant in transport terms: money is a measure of need.

Within the last few years, the objectives of Green Line have been sharply identified. Long-established services (Gravesend to Ascot, for example) have been withdrawn and resources diverted to routes that centre on London Airport and provide a facility that rail cannot match (except for the journey from Central London to

Below: The arrival of Green Line at the heart of Heathrow in 1967 was the beginning of a major shift of interest. RP coaches took over the 727 on 18 December 1971. This is RP84 pausing at London Airport Central. *Edward Shirras*

Above: Current Green Line practice and hopes are based on the new RB and RS coaches. Here RB52 works a 718 journey from Windsor to Victoria, a route with considerable tourist potential. The whole system now displays a confidence lacking for many years. *Edward Shirras*

Heathrow of course, where Green Line has arrived some 25 years too late.) Market research on such routes as the new 707 (Luton to Victoria) has identified need and the coaches are well-filled. The new 702 running from Bishops Stortford to Walthamstow provides an excellent example of a fast road service connecting directly with an Underground route to Central London. The tedious road journey to the centre is thus no longer a part of the operation and the coaches are able to keep much more closely to their schedules. There have been many suggestions for such arrangements in the past, though the model appeared as long ago as 1929 with the opening of the Watford to Golders Green service. It seems essential in the whole process of clarifying aims that Green Line had to abandon what had become a loss-making, cumbersome system. It was necessary to place resources where they would be most useful and, hopefully, attract new traffic to reorganised services. It is probable that the bus and coach industry has reached a plateau after the long decline; a period of stability would allow some estimate to be made of the viability of services operated. To all levels, from management to drivers, the sight of near-empty vehicles ponderously maintaining scheduled journeys that no one seems to need any more is a depressing experience. A full vehicle is a tonic in itself, an expression of usefulness. The long arm of

the past hung over Green Line operations too long; only recently have initiatives been taken that promise something for the future.

Green Line has become an institution, as much part of the London scene as the familiar red bus. It has meant over the years a special category of travel that is available nowhere else – the diagonal route systems were never emulated even in Birmingham and Manchester where there was some development of express working. The service undoubtedly had character; it was always much more personal than train-travel. There is still an element of myth about it – who except the eccentric are going to travel from Tunbridge Wells to London in two hours and seven minutes when the corresponding rail facility (on equal frequency) takes 50 minutes? Did anyone travel from Aylesbury to East Grinstead? Quite clearly, demand is for journeys over much shorter distances, passengers heading for such suburban centres as Kingston and Brent Cross. Their requirement is for reliable, comfortable and convenient travel. The recent changes in Green Line thinking thus accept local needs and tailor services to meet them; there is no longer the concept of the system as established in the 1933 map. There has been a radical change in organisational structure in the service and new opportunities have arisen as a result. Those whose professional and personal regard for Green Line has been of long-standing will hope that the green coach with yellow destination blinds will not become a museum piece but will continue as an important contributor to London's travel facilities.

Appendices

1 November 1930: Projected Scheme for through-London Working

Gravesend (60) Dartford (30) Staines – Windsor
Farningham (60)⎫
Sidcup (60)　　⎬Lewisham (15) Slough – Windsor
Orpington (30)⎭
Sevenoaks (30) London – Gerrards Cross (60) West Wycombe *and* (60) Amersham
Sevenoaks (60) Westerham Hill (30) London – Maidenhead
Tunbridge Wells (30) London – Uxbridge
Edenbridge (60) Chelsham (30) London – Gerrards Cross (60) Beaconsfield and (60) Amersham
Caterham on the Hill (60) London – Uxbridge
Caterham on the Hill (60) London – Harrow Weald
Redhill (30) London – Northwood (60) Chesham
East Grinstead (60) Godstone (30) London – Two Waters (60) Hemel Hempstead and (60)
Tring (120) Wendover
Belmont (30) London – Watford
Oxted (60) Chelsham (30) London – Watford
Reigate (30) London – Baldock
Dorking (30) London – St Albans (60) Dunstable and (60) Wheathampstead
Guildford (30) London – Bishops Stortford*
Chertsey (30) London – Ware (60) Hertford and (60) Royston*
Byfleet (30) London – Ongar
*Original proposals were Guildford (30) London – Ware (60) Hertford and (60) Royston;
Chertsey (30) London – Bishops Stortford changed to avoid competing with Skylark Guildford to
London and Hertford service. It will be noted that Ascot and Sunningdale appear to have been
forgotten.

2 Green Line routes operating immediately before the opening of Poland Street 24 December 1930

From Oxford Circus
Redhill (Every 30 minutes), Crawley (60)
Tunbridge Wells (30)
Sevenoaks via Westerham (60)
Godstone Green (30)
Chelsham (30), Edenbridge (60)
East Grinstead (60)
Dorking (30)

These services were East Surrey operations, although the Tunbridge Wells route was worked by Autocar.

From Charing Cross (Embankment)
Brentwood (15)　　　　Green Line
Ascot (60)　　　　　　Green Line
Sunningdale (60)　　　Green Line

Chertsey (30)	Green Line	
Tring (30)	Green Line	
Watford (30)	Green Line ex-LGOC	
Guildford (30)	Green Line	
Hertford (60)	National	
Windsor via Staines (30)	Green Line ex-LGOC	
Windsor via Slough (15)	Green Line ex-LGOC	
Maidenhead (30)	Green Line ex-LGOC	
Bishops Stortford (30)	National	

Through Services

Reigate (30) Welwyn Garden City East Surrey and National (via Northumberland Avenue and Oxford Circus)

Great Bookham (30) Harpenden East Surrey and Green Line (via Northumberland Avenue and Oxford Circus)

3 The First Lettering Scheme of 21 February 1931

Services from Poland Street

C	Chertsey
D	Dorking
F	Hertford
G	Guildford
I	Farningham
J	Edenbridge
L	Tunbridge Wells
M	Maidenhead
N	Windsor via Staines
P	Rickmansworth
Q	Uxbridge
S	Sunbury Common
U	East Grinstead
X	Sevenoaks via Westerham
Y	West Byfleet

Services from Embankment

B	Brentwood
O	Bishops Stortford
W	Watford
Z	Windsor via Slough

AV   Upminster via Barking

Through Services

A	Ascot/Sunningdale – Northumberland Avenue – Dartford
E	Bushey – Oxford Circus – Crawley
H	Harpenden – Oxford Circus – Great Bookham
K	Hemel Hempstead – Oxford Circus – Caterham
R	Hitchin – Oxford Circus – Reigate
T	Aylesbury – Oxford Circus – Godstone Green

Out-London Service

V   Golders Green – Watford

Note: at the direction of the Minister of Transport, AV was withdrawn and T altered to run from Tring to Godstone Green on 1 April 1931.

4 Licences

Green Line sought licences for the scheme listed in Appendix 3 and made the following proposals to the Traffic Commissioners:

1) Reinstate	T	to Aylesbury
	AV	(Embankment to Upminster via Barking)
2) Introduce	AU	(Embankment to Upminster via Ilford)
	new Y	Woking – Weybridge – London

3) Extend	E	to Watford
	H	to Luton and to Guildford
	AH	to Dunstable and to Guildford
	P	to Chesham
	AQ	(part of Q) to High Wycombe
	AR	(part of R) to Baldock
	Y	to Woking (and relettered AG)

None of these proposals was accepted, except for Woking to Weybridge, and the extension to Dunstable. In addition Green Line lost the following:

E   Section Bushey to London
M   Poland Street to Maidenhead
T   Section Godstone to London
Z   Poland Street to Windsor

However, they acquired the following routes (all with licences) between 21 February 1931 and 4 October 1933:

ACME   Charing Cross – Bishops Stortford (Acme)
AF   Oxford Circus – Hertford Heath (Skylark)

CF   Oxford Circus – Hertford (Regent)
BG   Oxford Circus – Guildford (Skylark)
AO   Bishopsgate – Ongar (Associated)
AQ   Oxford Circus – High Wycombe (Skylark)
AR   Kings Cross – Baldock (Queen Line)
AT   Marble Arch – Aylesbury (Red Rover)
AU   Paddington – East Grinstead (Blue Belle)
AW   Oxford Circus – Watford (Bucks Express)

Green Line also acquired BR Charing Cross – Brookman's Park, but the service did not survive long enough to be written into the 4 October scheme.

5 Second Allocation of Route Letters 4 October 1933

A   Gravesend – Ascot
AA   Gravesend – Sunningdale
B   Wrotham – Rickmansworth
C   Tunbridge Wells – Chertsey
AC   Tunbridge Wells – Woking
D   Sevenoaks – Sunbury Common
E   Edenbridge – Tring
F   Tatsfield – Hemel Hempstead
AF   Marylebone – Hemel Hempstead
G   Caterham – Horse Guards Avenue
H   East Grinstead – Harpenden
AH   East Grinstead – Dunstable
BH   Reserved for: Kings Cross – Luton (acqd 1/2/34)
I   Crawley – Watford
J   Reigate – Watford
K   Dorking – Hitchin
AK   Kings Cross – Baldock
L   Great Bookham – Uxbridge
M   Guildford – Hertford via Enfield
AM   Guildford – Hertford via Great Cambridge Road
BM   West Byfleet – Hertford via Great Cambridge Road

N   Windsor – Epping
O   Reserved for: Windsor – Cockspur Street (acqd 20/12/33)
P   Reserved for: Farnham Common – Cockspur Street (acqd 20/12/33)
Q   High Wycombe – Oxford Circus
R   Amersham – Oxford Circus
S   Reserved for: Aylesbury – Victoria (acqd 17/1/34)
T   Watford – Golders Green
U   Marylebone – Whipsnade
V   Bishops Stortford – Horse Guards Avenue
W   Ongar – Liverpool Street
X   Reserved for: Gidea Park – Horse Guards Avenue (started 25/10/33)
Y   Brentwood – Horse Guards Avenue
AY   Reserved for: Upminster – Aldgate (acqd 10/1/34)
Z   Reserved for Tilbury – Aldgate (acqd 23/12/33)
AZ   Reserved for Aveley – East Ham (acqd 1/12/33)

6 Green Line Services as listed in the No 1 Green Line Coach Guide, February 1936

A1	Gravesend (60) Ascot via Victoria
A2	Gravesend (60) Sunningdale via Victoria
B	Wrotham (60) Wendover (120) Aylesbury
C1	Tunbridge Wells (60) Chertsey
C2	Tunbridge Wells (60) Woking
D	Sevenoaks (60) Westerham Hill (30) Staines
E	Chelsham (60) Tring (120, 60sso) Aylesbury
F	Edenbridge (120) Hemel Hempstead
	Tatsfield (120) Hemel Hempstead
G	Caterham Station (60) Horse Guards Avenue
H1	East Grinstead (60) Luton, via Felbridge
H2	East Grinstead (60) Dunstable, via Baldwyns Hill
BH	Luton (30) King's Cross, via Barnet
I	Crawley (60) Redhill (30) Watford (60) Abbots Langley
J	Reigate (30) Watford
K1	Baldock (60) Leatherhead, via Potters Bar
	Welwyn Garden City (60) Dorking, via Potters Bar
K2	Hitchin (60sso) Welwyn Garden City (60) Dorking (120) Horsham
L	Uxbridge (30) Leatherhead (60, 30sso) Great Bookham
M1	Hertford (30) Guildford, via Enfield
M2	Hertford (60) West Byfleet Corner, via Hertford Heath and Turkey Street
M3	Hertford (60) Esher (60sso) Guildford, via Turkey Street
N	Windsor (30) Epping (60sso) Bishops Stortford, via Staines
O	Windsor (20/15) Trafalgar Square, via Slough
P	Farnham Common (60/30) Trafalgar Square, via Slough
Q	High Wycombe (60) Oxford Circus
R	Chesham (60) Oxford Circus
T1	Watford (60) Golders Green, via Brockley Hill
T2	Watford (60) Golders Green, via Elstree
U	Marylebone (irregular) Whipsnade Zoo
V	Bishops Stortford (30) Liverpool Street (30*) Horse Guards Avenue
W	Ongar (30) Liverpool Street
X	Gidea Park (15) Aldgate (15*) Horse Guards Avenue, via Eastern Avenue
Y1	Brentwood (15/7) Romford (7/3) Aldgate (30/15*) Horse Guards Avenue
Y2	Corbets Tey (15/10) Aldgate
	Hornchurch Station (15/10) Aldgate
Z1	Tilbury (60) Grays (30/20) Aldgate via Purfleet Station
Z2	Grays (60) Aldgate, via Aveley and Wennington

Note: *The extensions to Horse Guards Avenue applied late pm Mondays to Fridays, Saturdays pm and all day Sundays, with certain exceptions.

By August 1939, the following changes had been made:

D	Westerham (60) Westerham Hill (30) Staines
G	Caterham (30) London (15/20) Windsor via Slough
BH	now H3
K3	Horsham (120/60) Dorking – Baker Street via Kingston
L	withdrawn
O	withdrawn
T	Watford (30) Golders Green via Brockley Hill
V, X, Y1	– all curtailed at Aldgate

7 Emergency Bus Routes, 1939–1940

Emergency Bus Routes commencing 1 September 1939

369	St Albans – Dunstable
371	Grays – East Ham, via Aveley
371A	Grays – East Ham, via by-pass
380A	Broxbourne – Hertford via Hertford Heath
392	Woodford Wells – Ongar
393	Amersham – Great Missenden
396	Epping – Bishops Stortford
403C	Warlingham – Tatsfield
403D	Sevenoaks – Tunbridge Wells
465	Warlingham – Edenbridge
478	Swanley – Wrotham

Additional journeys were also operated on 455 (Uxbridge – High Wycombe).

The services listed above were subsequently modified: on 6 December 1939 route 392 was withdrawn between Woodford Wells and Epping; on 1 January 1940 route 478 was altered to run Horton Kirby to Wrotham.

8 Emergency Arrangements commencing 4 December 1940

New Services

Old Letter	New Number	Route	Basic Headway
B	3	Victoria – Wrotham	60
B	35	Victoria – Aylesbury	60
E/F	40B	Victoria – Watford	30
H3	46	Victoria – Luton, via Barnet and Golders Green	30
I	9 ⎱	Oxford Circus – Crawley	60
	⎰	Oxford Circus – Redhill	30
J	10	Oxford Circus – Reigate	30
M1/3	18	Oxford Circus – Guildford	30
V	53	Aldgate – Bishops Stortford	30

Revised Services

Old Letter	New Number	Route	Basic Headway
A	2	Victoria – Gravesend	30
C	5	Victoria – Tunbridge Wells	30
H1	8	Victoria – East Grinstead	30
C1	20	Victoria – Chertsey	30
A1	23	Victoria – Ascot	60
A2	23A	Victoria – Sunningdale	60
E	40	Victoria – Aylesbury	30
F	40A	Victoria – Hemel Hempstead	30
H1	45	Victoria – Luton, via Radlett	30
Q	33	Oxford Circus – High Wycombe	30
R	34 ⎱	Oxford Circus – Chesham	60
	⎰	Oxford Circus – Amersham	60
M	49	Oxford Circus – Hertford	20
N	52	Oxford Circus – Epping	30
Y1	55 ⎱	Aldgate – Brentwood	30
	⎰	Aldgate – Romford	6–15
Z1	59	Aldgate – Grays	20–30
Z2	59A	Aldgate – Grays, via Aveley	20–30

Emergency Arrangement commencing 18 December 1940

New Services

Old Letter	New Number	Route	Basic Headway
K1	14	Victoria – Dorking, via Epsom	30
K3	15	Victoria – Dorking, via Kingston	30
D	25	Victoria – Staines, via Kingston	30
G	26	Victoria – Windsor, via Slough	20
P	26A	Victoria – Farnham Common	60
K1	47	Victoria – Hitchin	60
	47A	Victoria – Welwyn Garden City	60
X	54	Aldgate – Romford, via Eastern Avenue	20–30

Revised Service

Y2	56	Aldgate – Corbets Tey	30
		Aldgate – Hornchurch	10–15

Notes: 40B never ran; 25 actually operated as 21, 56 as 58.

9 1946 Numbering Scheme

701 Gravesend (60) Ascot
702 Gravesend (60) Sunningdale
703 Wrotham (60) Amersham
704 Tunbridge Wells (30) Windsor
705 Sevenoaks (30) Windsor
706 Westerham (60) Aylesbury
707 Oxted (60) Aylesbury
708 East Grinstead (30) Hemel Hempstead
709 Caterham (60) Baker Street
710 Crawley (60) Baker Street
711 Reigate (30) Baker Street
712 Dorking (60) Luton
713 Dorking (60) Dunstable
714 Dorking (30) Baker Street via Kingston
715 Guildford (20) Hertford
716 Chertsey (60) Hitchin
717 Woking (60) Welwyn Garden City
718 Windsor (30) Epping
720 Bishops Stortford (30) Aldgate
721 Brentwood (10/20) Aldgate
722 Corbets Tey or Hornchurch (15) Aldgate
723 Tilbury (60) Grays (20) Aldgate
724 High Wycombe (30) Oxford Circus
725 Chesham (60) Amersham (30) Oxford Circus
726 Whipsnade (irregular) Marylebone
727 Luton (30) Kings Cross

Subsequently, 709 became Caterham (60) Chesham; 710 became Crawley (60) Amersham; 711 became Reigate (30) High Wycombe; 714 became Dorking (30) Luton; allowing withdrawal of 724, 725 and 727 as route numbers. Confirmation for the reason why there was no route 719 cannot be found, although one explanation might be that it was intended for Farnham Common.

New routes that appeared between 1951 and 1962:

715A Hertford (60) Marble Arch
719 Hemel Hempstead (30/60) Victoria
720A Harlow New Town (60) Aldgate
723A Tilbury – Grays (30) Aldgate via Belhus Park Estate
725 Gravesend (60) Dartford (30) Croydon – Staines – Windsor

Between 1962 and 1969 the following appeared:

724 Romford (60) Hertford – St Albans – Watford – High Wycombe
727 Luton (60) Watford – London Airport – Reigate – Crawley

The number 727 had also been used for the short-lived Tring to Victoria express service.

10 Allocation of Vehicles, 1 July 1962

At this date, the Green Line operation was at its most extensive in the postwar period. The fleet was standardised on the RF coach and the RT double-deck vehicle. A feature of the time was the provision of duplicate coaches on Mondays to Fridays in the peak hours, and at weekends, especially on Sunday evenings.

Garage		Service(s)	Basic Allocation	Duplicates
CM	Chelsham	706, 707	8 RF	1 RT
CY	Crawley	710	4 RF	3 RT
DG	Dunton Green	705	7 RF	1 RT
DS	Dorking	712, 713	7 RF	
		714	7 RF	1 RF or RT
DT	Dartford	725	3 RF	3 RF
EG	East Grinstead	708	7 RF	
EP	Epping	718	9 RF	2 RT
		720	7 RF	1 RT
		720A	3RF	
GD	Godstone	709	4 RF	2 RT
GF	Guildford	715	10 RF	1 RF or RT
GR	Garston	719	8 RF	1 RT
GY	Grays	723 series	18 RT	3 RT
HE	High Wycombe	711	7 RF	1 RF + 1 RT
HF	Hatfield	717	4 RF	1 RT
HG	Hertford	715	11 RF	5 RT
		715A	4 RF	2 RT
HH	Hemel Hempstead	708	6 RF	1 RF + 1 RT
LS	Luton	714	7 RF	1 RT
MA	Amersham	703	4 RF	1 RF
		709	3 RF	1 RT
		710	4 RF	
NF	Northfleet	701, 702	6 RF	2 RT
		725	4 RF	2 RF
RE	Romford	721, 722	29 RT	
		726	2 RT	
RG	Reigate	711	7 RF	2 RT
SA	St Albans	712, 713	7 RF	2 RF + 3 RT
SJ	Swanley	703	4 RF	3 RT
ST	Staines	701, 702	6 RF	2 RT
		725	7 RF	3 RF
SV	Stevenage	716, 716A	7 RF + 1 RMC	3 RT
TG	Tring	706, 707	8 RF	1 RT
TW	Tunbridge Wells	704	7 RF	1 RF
WR	Windsor	704	8 RF	5 RT
		705	6 RF	
		718	8 RF	2 RT
WY	Addlestone	716, 716A	7 RF	2 RT

Additionally, 1 RF was kept at Gillingham Street, Victoria (GM) and another at Hammersmith Riverside (R). These allocations give totals of:

244	RF
82	RT
1	RMC
327	vehicles

11 Green Line Routes on 1 January 1970 – the London Country Inheritance

701 Gravesend (60) Ascot
702 Gravesend (60 Saturdays & Sundays only) Sunningdale (Peak hour journeys only on Mondays to Fridays between Victoria and Sunningdale)
704 Tunbridge Wells (60) Windsor
705 Sevenoaks (60) Windsor via Westerham
706 Aylesbury (30) Chelsham, with some extensions to Westerham
708 Hemel Hempstead (60) East Grinstead
709 Godstone – Baker Street
(Monday to Friday peak and Sunday journeys only)
710 Amersham (60) Baker Street
711 High Wycombe (60) Reigate
(Every 30 minutes on Saturdays)
712 Dorking (120, 60 on Saturdays) Dunstable via Park Street
713 Dorking (120) Dunstable via Shenley
(On Saturdays, every 60 minutes between Dorking & St Albans)
714 Dorking (60) Luton via Kingston
715 Guildford (60, 30 on Saturdays) Oxford Circus (30) Hertford
716 Chertsey (60) Hitchin via Brookmans Park
716A Woking (60) Stevenage via Welham Green
718 Windsor (60) Harlow via Kingston & Chingford
719 Hemel Hempstead (60) Wrotham
(with supplementary journeys between Garston and Victoria)
720 Bishops Stortford (60) Aldgate
(with supplementary journeys between Harlow and Aldgate)
721 Brentwood (12 to 20) Aldgate
723 Tilbury (60) Grays (30) Aldgate
724 High Wycombe (60) Romford
725 Gravesend (60) Dartford (30) Windsor via Croydon
727 Luton (60) Crawley via London Airport

Note: 706 was licensed to run to Chartwell in the Summer months; 712 and 713 journeys were worked to Whipsnade.

12 London Country Summer 1979 Green Line Route Numbers

*denotes numbers surviving from the 1946 scheme

700 Windsor (60) Victoria (Summer express only)
701 Windsor (60) Victoria, semi-fast via Slough
702 Bishops Stortford (60) Walthamstow
*704 Windsor (60) Victoria via Slough
*705 Tunbridge Wells – Westerham – Victoria (120, Sundays only)
706 Tunbridge Wells – Farnborough – Victoria (60, 120 on Sundays)
707 Luton (60 with 717 below) Victoria
*708 Aylesbury – Hemel Hempstead (60) Victoria
*709 Godstone (peak hour & Sunday journeys only) Baker Street
710 Guildford (peak hour express journeys) Oxford Circus
712 Bishops Stortford (60 with 713) Romford
713 Bishops Stortford (60 with 712) Romford via Chigwell
*714 Dorking – Kingston (60) Victoria
*715 Guildford (60 with supplementary journeys) Hertford
*716 Woking (60) or Staines (Sundays only) Oxford Circus
*718 Windsor (60) Victoria via Kingston
719 Hemel Hempstead (60) Victoria – East Grinstead

722	Hitchin (60 with 732 below) Victoria	
*723	Grays (30) Aldgate	
724	Windsor (60) Harlow, peripheral route	
725	Windsor (60) Gravesend, peripheral route	
726	Windsor (60) Gravesend, peripheral route via Heathrow	
727	Crawley (60) Reigate (30) Heathrow (60) Luton Airport	
729	Borough Green (peak hour journeys only) Victoria	
732	Hitchin (60 with 722) Victoria via Brent Cross	
737	Whipsnade Zoo (special journeys) Victoria	
739	Brands Hatch (special journeys) Victoria	
747	Gatwick (60, non-stop) Heathrow (Jet Link)	
790	Amersham (120) Victoria	

13 Allocation of Vehicles, 1 August 1979

Garage		Service(s)	Allocation
DG	Dunton Green	705, 706	6 RB
DS	Dorking	714	4 SNC (to be RB/RS)
DT	Dartford	725	4 RB
EG	East Grinstead	719	5 SNC (to be RB/RS)
GD	Godstone	709	2 SNC
GF	Guildford	710	2 RS
		715	7 RS
GR	Garston	719	3 SNC (to be RB/RS)
GY	Grays	723	10 SNC
HA	Harlow	702, 712, 713	7 RP
		724	3 RB
HF	Hatfield	722/732	4 RS
HG	Hertford	715	9 RS
HH	Hemel Hempstead	708	8 RS
MA	Amersham	790	2 RB
NF	Northfleet	725, 726	6 RB
RG	Reigate	727	8 RS + 1 RS and 1 SNC for late-running coaches
SA	St Albans	707, 717	5 RS + 1 SNC late-running coach
		727	4 RS + 1 RS late-running coach
		737	1 RS (included in 707/717 alloc'n)
SJ	Swanley	729	1 SNC
ST	Staines	718	4 RB
		724	4 RB
		747	4 RB
SV	Stevenage	722/732	2 RS
WR	Windsor	700	2 RB
		701, 704	8 RB
		725, 726	8 RB + 1 RB late-running coach
WY	Addlestone	716	6 RB

Totals

120	RB/RS
8	RP
15	SNC
143	vehicles

Bibliography

The most authoritative presentation of the historical background relevant to this study of Green Line will be found in T. C. Barker and Michael Robbins: *A History of London Transport, Volume II*; Allen and Unwin, 1974. Especially interesting are the appendices (Appendix 3 deals in detail with *London Area Omnibus Proprietors. 1920 – 1933*) and the notes on the Chapters. General background to the development of coach work is provided in L. A. G. Strong: *The Rolling Road*, Hutchinson, 1956, though in very general terms. More academically satisfying is John Hibbs' *The Bus and Coach Industry, Its Economics and Organisation*, Dent, 1975, a book of great value, sadly discovered remaindered for 50p on a bookstall at Liverpool Street. O. J. Morris: *Fares Please*, Ian Allan, 1953, gives the story of London's road transport up to that date; wartime activity is dealt with in C. Graves: *London Transport Carries On*, LPTB, 1947 – there are some references to Green Line, but not many. J. S. Wagstaff: *The London Country Bus*, Oakwood Press, 1968, includes some material on early Green Line development. Recent publications by the London Omnibus Traction Society (LOTS), especially their annual reviews, are most informative and helpful.

A most important source of detail on early Green Line is a paper presented by E. N. Osborne to the Omnibus Society: *The Ancestry and History of Green Line Coaches*, 1953, later published by Ian Allan in *Buses and Trams*. Subsequent development can be traced through London Transport Reports, the now defunct weekly *Modern Transport, Buses*, formerly *Buses Illustrated*, fortunately still with us, and the *London Transport Magazine*. Much of this information is, of course, fragmentary; so far as London Transport was concerned, separate financial figures for Green Line were never published – one wonders why; National Bus Company Reports are similarly limited in the amount of detail offered. Vehicles are dealt with in considerable and interesting detail in J. Graeme Bruce and Colin H. Curtis: *The London Motor Bus: Its Origins and Development*, London Transport, 1973. This was followed by Colin H. Curtis: *Buses of London*, London Transport, 1977, which provides a brief historical review of every type of bus purchased by London Transport or its predecessors since 1905. There is similar concern for technical detail in two books by David Kaye: *Buses and Trolleybuses 1919–1945*, and *Buses and Trolleybuses Since 1945*, both published by Blandford Press, 1970 and 1968 respectively. J. S. Wagstaff: *The London Single Deck Bus of the Fifties*, Oakwood Press 1976, deals mainly with the RF. Reference must also be made to the London Buses handbooks published by Ian Allan; the first appeared in 1945 and was entitled *The ABC of London Transport Services* by Barrington Tatford. The most recent was published in 1980.

Government papers concerned with Green Line include the *Report of the Committee of Inquiry into London Motorcoach Services* (First Report June 1932, Second Report August 1932), a valuable source of information on early coach operations. Dissatisfaction with London Transport's performance led to the setting up of the Chambers Committee and the publication of the *Report of the Committee of Inquiry into London Transport*, HMSO 1955. This was a somewhat bland document which suggested that what was being done could not be done very much better. Of specific relevance to Green Line operation was the *Report of the Committee of Inquiry into the Pay and Conditions of Employment of the Drivers and Conductors of the London Transport Board Road Services*, HMSO 1964. Pay for Green Line crews who worked in both country and central areas was a pertinent problem. *Transport in London*, a White Paper presented by the Minister of Transport to Parliament in July 1967 heralded the transfer of much of London Transport's interests to the Greater London Council and Green Line's transfer to the National Bus Company.

A study of Green Line operation must rely very heavily on timetables, maps and publicity material. The leaflets and timetables of Green Line up to 1939 were kindly made available to me by the Librarian of the Omnibus Society when I began this research; subsequently I have depended on my own collection. In the end the most satisfying study of Green Line – or any other form of transport for that matter – must depend on knowledge of the timetables and actual travelling experience that indicates how they work.